"Nothing would h.   et
the words of the title in the right order. We are reading the Bible with
John Stott, not just reading John Stott on the Bible. For in his preaching
as in his writing, John Stott's greatest gift was to help people see and
hear clearly what the Bible itself actually says, and then, of course, to
challenge us as to how we should respond to what we see and hear. Not
all of us possess the complete works of John Stott. But we do possess
the complete Bible. These sensitively edited extracts from Stott's
writings will not only introduce new readers to the riches of his biblical
exposition (and make them hungry for more), but will surely also introduce them to riches of God's word they had not seen before."

Christopher J. H. Wright, international ministries director,
Langham Partnership

"No one I have known has loved, preached, taught and lived the Bible
any more than John Stott. He often quoted Spurgeon's comment that
we should seek for our very blood to become 'Bibline'; so seriously
should we soak in Scripture in order to know and live it. This new series
will give us daily help in just such living."

Mark Labberton, president, Fuller Theological Seminary, author of *Called*

"More than any other author, John Stott urges us to engage in double
listening. He wants us to listen to the Word God spoke and the world
God loves so that we apply the timeless truths of Scripture to the ever-
changing context of our life. To help us, he explains the Bible with
clarity, charity and humility. His writings propel us to Jesus and into
the mission of God in the world."

Greg Jao, vice president and director of campus engagement,
InterVarsity Christian Fellowship

READING

ROMANS

with

JOHN STOTT

VOLUME
2

WITH QUESTIONS FOR

GROUPS OR INDIVIDUALS

JOHN STOTT

with DALE & SANDY LARSEN

IVP Connect
An imprint of InterVarsity Press
Downers Grove, Illinois

InterVarsity Press
P.O. Box 1400, Downers Grove, IL 60515-1426
ivpress.com
email@ivpress.com

InterVarsity Press® is the book-publishing division of InterVarsity Christian Fellowship/USA®, a movement of students and faculty active on campus at hundreds of universities, colleges and schools of nursing in the United States of America, and a member movement of the International Fellowship of Evangelical Students. For information about local and regional activities, visit intervarsity.org.

Cover design: Cindy Kiple
Interior design: Beth McGill
Images: © Yolande de Kort / Trevillion Images

ISBN 978-0-8308-3192-0 (print)
ISBN 978-0-8308-9333-1 (digital)

Printed in the United States of America ♾

Library of Congress Cataloging-in-Publication Data

Names: Stott, John R. W., author. | Larsen, Dale, author. | Larsen, Sandy, author. | Stott, John R. W. Message of Romans.
Title: Reading Romans with John Stott / John Stott with Dale and Sandy Larsen ; with questions for groups or individuals.
Description: Downers Grove : InterVarsity Press, 2016. | Series: Reading the Bible with John Stott (RBJS) | "Vol. 1." | "This volume is abridged and edited from The Message of Romans..." | Includes bibliographical references.
Identifiers: LCCN 2016011664 (print) | LCCN 2016017713 (ebook) | ISBN 9780830831913 (pbk. : alk. paper) | ISBN 9780830893324 (eBook)
Subjects: LCSH: Bible. Romans, I-VIII--Devotional literature.
Classification: LCC BS2665.54 .S76 2016 (print) | LCC BS2665.54 (ebook) | DDC 227/.107--dc23
LC record available at https://lccn.loc.gov/2016011664

P	21	20	19	18	17	16	15	14	13	12	11	10	9	8	7	6	5	4	3	2	1
Y	34	33	32	31	30	29	28	27	26	25	24	23	22	21	20	19	18	17	16

Contents

How to Read the Bible
with John Stott

❦

During John Stott's life from 1921 to 2011, he was one of the world's master Bible teachers. Christians on every continent heard and read John Stott's exposition of Scripture, which was at once instructive and inspiring. With over eight million copies of his over fifty books sold in dozens of languages, it is not surprising that *Time* magazine recognized him in 2005 as one of the "100 Most Influential People in the World" and *Christianity Today* called him "evangelicalism's premier teacher and preacher." At the core of his ministry was the Bible and his beloved Bible Speaks Today series, which he originated as New Testament series editor. He himself contributed several volumes to the series, which have now been edited for this Reading the Bible with John Stott series.

The purpose of this volume is to offer excerpts of Stott's *The Message of Romans* in brief readings, suitable for daily use. Though Stott was himself an able scholar, this series avoids technicalities and scholarly debates, with each reading emphasizing the substance, significance and application of the text.

Following each set of six readings is a discussion guide. This can be used by individuals to help them dig more deeply into the text. It can also be used by study groups meeting regularly. Individuals in the groups can go through the six readings between group meetings and then use the discussion guide to help the group understand and apply the Scripture passage. Discussions are designed to last between forty-five and sixty minutes. Guidelines for leaders at the end of this volume offer many helpful suggestions for having a successful meeting.

If you are a group member, you can help everyone present in the following ways:

1. Read and pray through the readings before you meet.

2. Be willing to participate in the discussion. The leader won't be lecturing. Instead all will be asked to discuss what they have learned.

3. Stick to the topic being discussed and focus on the particular passage of Scripture. Only rarely should you refer to other portions of the Bible or outside sources. This will allow everyone to participate on equal footing.

4. Listen attentively to what others have to say. Be careful not to talk too much but encourage a balanced discussion among all participants. You may be surprised by what you can learn from others. Generally questions do not have one right answer but are intended to explore various dimensions of the text.

5. Expect God to teach you through the passage and through what others have to say.

6. Use the following guidelines and read them at the start of the first session:

- We will make the group a safe place by keeping confidential what is said in the group about personal matters.

- We will provide time for each person to talk who wants to.

- We will listen attentively to each other.

- We will talk about ourselves and our own situations, avoiding conversation about others.

- We will be cautious about giving advice to one another.

John Stott had an immense impact on the church in the last half of the twentieth century. With these volumes readers today can continue to benefit from the riches of the Bible that Stott opened to millions.

Introduction

❦

Ever since I became a Christian, I have enjoyed a love-hate relationship with Romans because of its joyful-painful personal challenges. It began soon after my conversion, with my longing to experience that death to sin which Romans 6 seemed to promise. I toyed for many years with the fantasy that Christians are supposed to be as insensitive to sin as a corpse is to external stimuli. My final deliverance from this illusion was sealed when I gave a series of talks on Romans 5–8. Next, Paul's devastating exposure of universal human sin and guilt in Romans 1:18–3:20 rescued me from that superficial evangelism which is preoccupied only with people's "felt needs." Then there was Romans 12 and its demand for our wholehearted commitment in response to God's mercies, and Romans 13, whose teaching about the use of force in the administration of justice made it impossible for me to remain a total pacifist. As for Romans 8, although I have declaimed its final triumphant verses at innumerable funerals, I have never lost the thrill of them.

Paul, although a man of his age who addressed his contemporaries, also speaks to all people of every age. I have not been

surprised to observe how many contemporary issues Paul
touches on in Romans: enthusiasm for evangelism in general
and the propriety of Jewish evangelism in particular; whether
homosexual relationships are natural or unnatural; whether we
can still believe in such unfashionable concepts as God's wrath
and propitiation; the historicity of Adam's fall and the origin of
human death; the fundamental means to living a holy life; the
place of law and of the Spirit in Christian discipleship; the distinction between assurance and presumption; the relation between divine sovereignty and human responsibility in salvation;
the tension between ethnic identity and the solidarity of the
body of Christ; relations between church and state; the re-
spective duties of the individual citizen and the body politic; and
how to handle differences of opinion within the Christian community. And this list is only a sample of the modern questions
which, directly or indirectly, Romans raises and addresses.

Paul probably wrote the letter to the Romans from Corinth
during the three months he spent in Greece (Acts 20:2). He
mentions three places which he intends to visit: Jerusalem,
Rome and Spain. Paul thought of Rome, being situated between
Jerusalem and Spain, as a place of refreshment after he had been
to Jerusalem and a place of preparation en route for Spain. His
visits to Jerusalem and Spain were of special significance to him
because they expressed his two continuing commitments: to the
welfare of Israel (Jerusalem) and to the Gentile mission (Spain).

We still have to ask why Paul should write to the church in
Rome. It was partly to prepare them for his visit. More than that,
because he had not visited Rome before, and because most of the

church members there were not known to him, he saw the need to establish his apostolic credentials by giving a full account of his gospel. With regard to his own situation, he sent them a threefold request—to pray that his service in Jerusalem would be acceptable, to help him on his way to Spain and to receive him during his stopover in Rome as the apostle to the Gentiles.

Paul's purposes in writing to the Romans are traceable not only to his own situation, however. His letter also arose from the situation in which the Roman Christians found themselves.

The church in Rome was a mixed community consisting of both Jews and Gentiles, with Gentiles in the majority, and there was considerable conflict between these groups. This conflict was primarily not ethnic (different races and cultures) but theological (different convictions about the status of God's covenant and law, and so about salvation). This controversy may be heard rumbling through Romans. And Paul is seen from beginning to end as an authentic peacemaker, anxious to preserve both truth and peace without sacrificing either to the other. As a patriotic Jew who had been specially commissioned as apostle to the Gentiles, he was in a unique position to be an agent of reconciliation. He was determined to make a full and fresh statement of the apostolic gospel, which would not compromise any of its revealed truths, but which would at the same time resolve the conflict between Jews and Gentiles over the covenant and the law, and so promote the unity of the church.

In his ministry of reconciliation, Paul develops two paramount themes and interweaves them beautifully. The first is the justification of guilty sinners by God's grace alone in Christ alone through faith alone, irrespective of either status or works. This is the most humbling and leveling of all Christian truths and experiences, and so is the fundamental basis of Christian unity. Paul's second theme is the consequent redefinition of the people of God, no longer according to descent, circumcision or culture, but according to faith in Jesus, so that all believers are the true children of Abraham, regardless of their ethnic origin or religious practice.

In writing on Romans, my first responsibility has been to seek a fresh encounter with the authentic Paul. My aim is to allow the apostle to say what he does say and not force him to say what we might want him to say.

At the beginning of his fourth-century exposition of Romans, Chrysostom spoke of how much he enjoyed hearing Paul's "spiritual trumpet." My prayer is that we may hear it again in our day and may readily respond to its summons.

John Stott

1

Romans 9

Understanding God's Purposes

❧

A Threefold Affirmation

ROMANS 9:1-5

> [1]I speak the truth in Christ—I am not lying, my conscience confirms it through the Holy Spirit—[2]I have great sorrow and unceasing anguish in my heart. [3]For I could wish that I myself were cursed and cut off from Christ for the sake of my people, those of my own race, [4]the people of Israel. Theirs is the adoption to sonship; theirs the divine glory, the covenants, the receiving of the law, the temple worship and the promises. [5]Theirs are the patriarchs, and from them is traced the human ancestry of the Messiah, who is God over all, forever praised! Amen.

Chapters 9, 10 and 11 each begin with an expression of Paul's profound concern for the people of Israel. Here Paul offers a strong threefold affirmation, intended to put his sincerity beyond question and to persuade his readers to believe him.

First, "I speak the truth in Christ." Paul is conscious of his relationship to Christ and of Christ's presence with him as he writes. Second, as a negative counterpart, "I am not lying" or even exaggerating. Third, "my conscience confirms it through the Holy Spirit." Paul knows that the human conscience is fallible and culturally conditioned, but he claims that his is illumined by the Spirit of truth himself.

What is this truth that Paul asserts with such force? It concerns his continuing love for his people Israel who have rejected Christ. He goes on to call them "my people, those of my own race." Membership in the Christian community does not cancel our natural ties of family and nationality.

Paul boldly states that he could wish that for Israel's sake he himself were "cursed [*anathema*] and cut off from Christ." Paul is not literally expressing this wish, since he has already stated his conviction that nothing could ever separate him from God's love in Christ (Romans 8:35-39). He means that he could entertain such a wish, if it could possibly be granted.

The apostle's anguish over unbelieving Israel is the more poignant because of its unique privileges. Some of these he has mentioned earlier. Now he gives a fuller inventory. One would think that Israel, favored with all these blessings, prepared and educated for centuries for the arrival of its Messiah, would recognize and welcome him when he came. How can one reconcile Israel's privileges with its prejudices? How can one explain Israel's hardening against the gospel? This is the mystery that Paul will next address.

God's Word Has Not Failed

ROMANS 9:6-13

> [6]It is not as though God's word had failed. For not all who are descended from Israel are Israel. [7]Nor because they are his descendants are they all Abraham's children. On the contrary, "It is through Isaac that your offspring will be reckoned." [8]In other words, it is not the children by physical descent who are God's children, but it is the children of the promise who are regarded as Abraham's offspring. [9]For this was how the promise was stated: "At the appointed time I will return, and Sarah will have a son."
>
> [10]Not only that, but Rebekah's children were conceived at the same time by our father Isaac. [11]Yet, before the twins were born or had done anything good or bad—in order that God's purpose in election might stand: [12]not by works but by him who calls—she was told, "The older will serve the younger." [13]Just as it is written: "Jacob I loved, but Esau I hated."

At first sight it would appear that God's promise to Israel had failed. God had promised to bless them, but they had forfeited his blessing through unbelief. Israel's failure was its own failure, however; it was not due to the failure of God's word. There have always been two Israels, those physically descended from Israel (Jacob) on the one hand, and his spiritual progeny on the other. God's promise was addressed to the latter, who had received it. The apostle has already made this distinction between those who were Jews outwardly, whose circumcision was in the body, and those who were Jews inwardly, who had received a circumcision of the heart by the Spirit.

Paul now refers to two well-known Old Testament situations in order to illustrate and prove his point. The first concerns Abraham's family. Just as not all who are descended from Israel are Israel, so not all who are descended from Abraham are "Abraham's children," his true offspring. Who can be designated "Abraham's offspring"? It is not "the children by physical descent" but "the children of the promise," who were born as a result of God's promise.

Paul turns to Isaac and his two sons, Jacob and Esau, for his second illustration. He shows that just as God chose Isaac, not Ishmael, to be the recipient of his promise, so he chose Jacob, not Esau. In this case it was even clearer that God's decision had nothing to do with any eligibility in the boys themselves, for there was nothing to distinguish them from one another. Isaac and Ishmael had different mothers, but Jacob and Esau had the same mother; in fact they were twins. Yet "before the twins were born or had done anything good or bad," God had made his decision and revealed it to their mother.

The rejected brothers, Ishmael and Esau, were both circumcised, and therefore in some sense they too were members of God's covenant and were both promised lesser blessings. Nevertheless, both stories illustrate the same key truth of "God's purpose in election." God's promise did not fail, but it was fulfilled only in the Israel within Israel.

Many mysteries surround the doctrine of election, but it is an indispensable foundation of Christian worship, in time and eternity. God's redeemed people will spend eternity worshiping him, humbling themselves before him in grateful adoration, ascribing their salvation to him and to the Lamb, and acknowledging that he alone is worthy to receive all praise, honor and glory. Why? Because our salvation is due entirely to his grace, will, initiative, wisdom and power.

The Mercy of God

ROMANS 9:14-18

[14]What then shall we say? Is God unjust? Not at all! [15]For he says to Moses,

> "I will have mercy on whom I have mercy,
>> and I will have compassion on whom I have
>> compassion."

[16]It does not, therefore, depend on human desire or effort, but on God's mercy. [17]For Scripture says to Pharaoh: "I raised you up for this very purpose, that I might display my power in you and that my name might be proclaimed in all the earth." [18]Therefore God has mercy on whom he wants to have mercy, and he hardens whom he wants to harden.

Granted that God's promise has not failed, but has been fulfilled in Abraham, Isaac and Jacob, and in their spiritual lineage, is not God's purpose in election intrinsically unjust? Is choosing some for salvation and passing by others a breach of elementary justice? Paul's immediate retort is "Not at all!"

Paul's way of defending God's justice is to proclaim his mercy. It sounds like a complete non sequitur, but it is not. It simply indicates that the question itself is misconceived, because the basis on which God deals savingly with sinners is not justice but mercy. For salvation does not depend on "human desire or effort," that is, on anything we want or strive for, "but on God's mercy."

Paul sees the divine words to Moses and to Pharaoh, both recorded in Exodus, as complementary. "God has mercy on whom he wants to have mercy" (the message to Moses), "and he hardens whom he wants to harden" (the message to Pharaoh). The Exodus account makes it plain that Pharaoh hardened his heart against God and refused to humble himself. God's hardening of him was a judicial act, abandoning him to his own stubbornness.

So God is not unjust. As Paul demonstrated in the early chapters of his letter, all human beings are sinful and guilty in God's sight, so that nobody deserves to be saved. If God hardens some, he is not being unjust, for that is what their sin deserves. If, on the other hand, he has compassion on some, he is not being unjust, for he is dealing with them in mercy.

The wonder is not that some are saved and others not, but that anybody is saved at all. For we deserve nothing at God's hand but judgment. If we receive what we deserve (judgment), or if we receive what we do not deserve (mercy), in neither case is God unjust. Therefore if anybody is lost, the blame is theirs, but if anybody is saved, the credit is God's. This paradox contains a mystery our present knowledge cannot solve, but it is consistent with Scripture, history and experience.

God's Great Patience

ROMANS 9:19-24

¹⁹One of you will say to me: "Then why does God still blame us? For who is able to resist his will?" ²⁰But who are you, a human being, to talk back to God? "Shall what is formed say to the one who formed it, 'Why did you make me like this?'" ²¹Does not the potter have the right to make out of the same lump of clay some pottery for special purposes and some for common use?

²²What if God, although choosing to show his wrath and make his power known, bore with great patience the objects of his wrath—prepared for destruction? ²³What if he did this to make the riches of his glory known to the objects of his mercy, whom he prepared in advance for glory—²⁴even us, whom he also called, not only from the Jews but also from the Gentiles?

Paul's response to his critic's two questions is to pose three counterquestions that all concern our identity. They ask whether we know who we are, what kind of relationship we think exists between us and God, and what attitude to him we consider appropriate to this relationship. All three counterquestions emphasize the yawning gulf between human beings and God. Do we really think it is fitting for a human being to "talk back to God," for art to ask the artist why it has been made as it has, or for a pot to challenge the potter's right to shape the same lump of clay into pottery for different uses?

Paul does not wish to stifle genuine questions. After all, he has been asking and answering questions throughout the whole letter. Rather he censures the person who quarrels with God. Such a person manifests a reprehensible spirit of rebellion, refusing to let God be God and refusing to acknowledge his or her true status as creature and sinner.

But human beings are not merely lumps of inert clay, and this passage well illustrates the danger of arguing from an analogy. To liken humans to pottery is to emphasize the disparity between us and God. But there is another strand in biblical teaching that affirms not our unlikeness but our likeness to God, because we have been created in his image and because we still bear it (though distorted) even since the fall. As God's image bearers, we are rational, responsible, moral and spiritual beings, able to converse with God and encouraged to explore his revelation, to ask questions and to think his thoughts after him.

Paul's emphasis here is that as the potter has the right to shape the clay into vessels for different purposes, so God has the right to deal with fallen humanity according to both his wrath and his mercy. The apostle demonstrates that God's freedom to show mercy to some and to harden others is fully compatible with his justice. We must allow God to be God, not only renouncing every presumptuous desire to challenge him but also assuming that his actions are always in harmony with his nature.

The revelation of God's wrath to the objects of his wrath is with a view to the revelation of his glory to the objects of his mercy. The preeminent disclosure will be of the riches of God's glory, and the glory of his grace will shine the more brightly against the somber background of his wrath. "Glory" is of course shorthand for the final destiny of the redeemed, in which the splendor of God will be shown to and in them, as first they and then the universe are transformed.

So God's two actions, summed up as showing mercy and hardening, have now been traced back to his character. He does what he does because he is who he is. Although this does not solve the ultimate mystery of why he prepares some people in advance for glory and allows others to prepare themselves for destruction, both are revelations of God, of his patience and wrath in judgment, and above all of his glory and mercy in salvation.

Inclusion and Reduction

ROMANS 9:25-29

25As he says in Hosea:

"I will call them 'my people' who are not my people;
and I will call her 'my loved one' who is not my
loved one,"

26and,

"In the very place where it was said to them,
'You are not my people,'
there they will be called 'children of the living
God.'"

27Isaiah cries out concerning Israel:

"Though the number of the Israelites be like the sand
by the sea,
only the remnant will be saved.
28For the Lord will carry out
his sentence on earth with speed and finality."

[29]It is just as Isaiah said previously:

> "Unless the Lord Almighty
>> had left us descendants,
> we would have become like Sodom,
>> we would have been like Gomorrah."

Paul is responding to the question "Why does God still blame us?" He gives another explanation, which is that God foretold these things in Scripture.

Paul quotes two texts from Hosea to explain God's amazing inclusion of the Gentiles. Then he quotes two texts from Isaiah to explain God's equally amazing reduction of Jewish inclusion to a remnant. In order to understand Paul's handling of these texts, we need to remember that, according to the New Testament, Old Testament prophecies often have a threefold fulfillment. The first is immediate and literal (in the history of Israel), the second intermediate and spiritual (in Christ and his church) and the third ultimate and eternal (in God's consummated kingdom).

The prophecy of Hosea takes the form of God's promise in mercy to overturn an apparently hopeless situation, to love again those he had declared unloved and to welcome again as his people those he had said were not his people. The immediate and literal application was to Israel in the eighth century BC, repudiated and judged by the Lord for apostasy but promised reconciliation and reinstatement. However, God's promise to Hosea's children has a further and gospel fulfillment in the inclusion of the Gentiles. Their inclusion is a marvelous reversal of fortunes by God's mercy.

Paul turns from Hosea to Isaiah, from the inclusion of the Gentiles to the exclusion of the Jews, apart from a remnant. The historical background to the two Isaiah texts is again one of national apostasy in the eighth century BC. God promised that the conquering nation of Assyria would be punished for its arrogance and that a believing remnant would return to the Lord.

The significance of both texts lies in their contrast between the majority and the minority. On the one hand, God has called us, not only from the Jews but also from the Gentiles. So there is a fundamental Jewish-Gentile solidarity in God's new society. On the other hand, there is a serious imbalance between the size of the Gentile participation and the size of the Jewish participation in the redeemed community. As Hosea prophesied, multitudes of Gentiles, formerly disenfranchised, have now been welcomed as the people of God. As Isaiah prophesied, however, the Jewish membership was only a remnant of the nation, so small in fact as to constitute not the inclusion of Israel but its exclusion, not its acceptance but its rejection.

And so the outsiders have been welcomed inside, the aliens have become citizens, and the strangers are now beloved members of the family.

The Stumbling Stone

ROMANS 9:30-33

30What then shall we say? That the Gentiles, who did not pursue righteousness, have obtained it, a righteousness that is by faith; 31but the people of Israel, who pursued the law as the way of righteousness, have not attained their goal. [32]Why not? Because they pursued it not by faith but as if it were by works. They stumbled over the stumbling stone.[33]As it is written:

> "See, I lay in Zion a stone that causes people to stumble
>   and a rock that makes them fall,
>   and the one who believes in him will never be put
>   to shame."

The situation Paul describes is completely topsy-turvy. To describe pagans as "not pursuing righteousness" is a major understatement. Most of them are godless and self-centered, going their own way, lovers of themselves, of money and pleasure, rather than lovers of God and of goodness. Nevertheless, they obtained what they did not pursue. Indeed, when they heard the gospel of justification by faith, the Holy Spirit worked in them so powerfully that they "laid hold" of it almost with violence, by faith.

On the other hand, Israel's pursuit of righteousness was almost proverbial. They were imbued with a religious and moral zeal that some would call fanaticism. But they did not arrive at righteousness because they were pursuing an impossible goal. Paul sets over against the Gentiles' "righteousness," which is by faith, what he calls "the law as the way of righteousness," that is, the Torah viewed as a law to be obeyed.

With regard to the Jews who did not arrive at righteousness, Paul attributes Israel's failure to its own folly: "because they pursued it not by faith [which is how the Gentiles laid hold of it] but as if it were by works," that is, as if the accumulation of works righteousness were God's way of salvation. So they stumbled over the stumbling stone. What Paul means by this is not in doubt, since he uses the same imagery elsewhere. It is the proclamation of Christ crucified.

Why do people stumble over the cross? Because it undermines our self-righteousness. If we could gain a righteous standing before God by our own obedience to his law, the cross would be superfluous. If we could save ourselves, why should Christ have bothered to die? The fact that Christ died for our sins is proof positive that we cannot save ourselves. But to make this humiliating confession is an intolerable offense to our pride. So instead of humbling ourselves, we stumble over the stumbling stone.

Everybody has to decide how to relate to this rock that God has laid down. There are only two possibilities. One is to bark our shins against him and so to stumble and fall. The other is to put our trust in him, to take him as the foundation of our lives and build on him.

Romans 9

....

DISCUSSION GUIDE

OPEN

Suppose a friend says to you, "I think your Christianity is much too exclusive. People travel on all kinds of spiritual journeys, and I think that God accepts them all." How would you respond?

STUDY

Read Romans 9.

1. What phrases here show the intensity of Paul's concern for the Jewish people (vv. 1-3)?

2. What privileges had God already granted the Jews (vv. 4-5)?

3. Four questions outline this chapter (see vv. 6 [a statement], 14, 19 and 30). How would you phrase each question?

4. When and why have you asked a question similar to one of these?

5. Focus on verses 6-13. Does being a descendant of Abraham guarantee a spot in God's family? Why or why not?

6. How do the examples of Moses, Pharaoh and a potter help answer the question about God's justice?

7. What examples do you see of God's wrath and his mercy in verses 22-24?

8. How had the prophets Hosea and Isaiah prepared the Jewish people for the possibility that belonging in God's family was not simply a matter of biological heritage (vv. 25-29)?

9. Focus on verses 30-33. What relationships do you see here between faith, works, Jews and Gentiles?

10. What do you learn about Jesus Christ from verse 33?

11. How have you seen Christ in one of the ways described here?

APPLY

1. This chapter speaks several times of God's mercy. When and how have you seen God's mercy at work?

2. Paul speaks of people who did not come into God's family because instead of trusting in the "rock," they stumbled over it (vv. 32-33). Who among your friends and family seem to have made that same mistake?

3. Mentally select one of these people who do not yet believe. Try to see Christianity from that person's point of view. How do you think he or she sees the Christian faith?

2

Romans 10
God's Grief

❦

Zeal Without Knowledge

ROMANS 10:1-4

> ¹Brothers and sisters, my heart's desire and prayer to God for the Israelites is that they may be saved. ²For I can testify about them that they are zealous for God, but their zeal is not based on knowledge. ³Since they did not know the righteousness of God and sought to establish their own, they did not submit to God's righteousness. ⁴Christ is the culmination of the law so that there may be righteousness for everyone who believes.

Paul has no doubt of the Israelites' religious sincerity. He knows from his own experience that "they are zealous for God." In his own preconversion life, he was obsessed with his religion, even to the point of persecuting Christians. So he knows what he is talking about when he says that the Israelites' zeal "is not based on knowledge." Sincerity is not enough, for we may be sincerely mistaken. Zeal without knowledge, commitment without reflection or enthusiasm without understanding all equal fanaticism, a horrid and dangerous state.

Paul's assertion that the Jews "did not know the righteousness of God" means that they had not yet learned the way of salvation, how the righteous God puts the unrighteous right with himself by bestowing on them a righteous status. This is "the righteousness of God" that is revealed in the gospel and is received by faith altogether apart from the law, as Paul has written earlier. The tragic consequence of the Jews' ignorance was that, recognizing their need of righteousness if they were ever to stand in God's righteous presence, they "sought to establish their own," and "they did not submit to God's righteousness."

This ignorance of the true way, and this tragic adoption of the false way, are by no means limited to Jewish people. They are widespread among religious people of all faiths, including professing Christians. All human beings, who know that God is righteous and they are not, naturally look around for a righteousness that might qualify them to stand in God's presence. There are only two possible options. The first is to attempt to establish our own righteousness by our good works and religious observances. But this effort is doomed to failure. The other way is to submit to God's righteousness by receiving it from him as a free gift through faith in Jesus Christ.

Christ is the "culmination," that is, the "end," of the law. The reason Christ has terminated the law is "so that there may be righteousness for everyone who believes." In regard to salvation, Christ and the law are incompatible alternatives. If righteousness is by the law, it is not by Christ, and if it is by Christ through faith, it is not by the law. Christ and the law are both objective realities, both revelations and gifts of God. But now that Christ has accomplished our salvation by his death and resurrection, he has terminated the law in that role. Paul's desire and prayer is that his fellow Jews will accept this gospel truth.

With Heart and Mouth

Romans 10:5-10

> [5]Moses writes this about the righteousness that is by the law: "The person who does these things will live by them." [6]But the righteousness that is by faith says: "Do not say in your heart, 'Who will ascend into heaven?'" (that is, to bring Christ down) [7]"or 'Who will descend into the deep?'" (that is, to bring Christ up from the dead). [8]But what does it say? "The word is near you; it is in your mouth and in your heart," that is, the message concerning faith that we proclaim: [9]If you declare with your mouth, "Jesus is Lord," and believe in your heart that God raised him from the dead, you will be saved. [10]For it is with your heart that you believe and are justified, and it is with your mouth that you profess your faith and are saved.

Paul has already stated three antitheses—between faith and works; between God's righteousness, to which we should submit, and our own righteousness, which we mistakenly seek to establish; and between Christ and the law. Now he draws out the implications by contrasting "the righteousness that is by the law" with "the righteousness that is by faith." He does so by appealing to Scripture, quoting Moses from Leviticus and Deuteronomy.

On the one hand, "Moses writes this about the righteousness that is by the law: 'The person who does these things will live by them.'" The natural interpretation of these words is that the way to life (that is, salvation) is by obedience to the law. But no one has succeeded in obeying it. The weakness of the law is our own weakness. Because we disobey it, instead of bringing us life it brings us under its curse, and that would still be our position if Christ had not redeemed us from the law's curse by becoming a curse for us.

On the other hand, "the righteousness that is by faith" proclaims a different message. It sets before us for salvation not the law but Christ, and it assures us that unlike the law, Christ is not unattainable but readily accessible. There is no need for us to scale the heights or plumb the depths in search of Christ, for he has already come, died and risen, and so is accessible to us. Taking his cue from the reference to the people's "mouth" and "heart" already quoted, Paul now summarizes the gospel: "If you declare with your mouth, 'Jesus is Lord' [the earliest and simplest of all Christian creeds] and believe in your heart that God raised him from the dead, you will be saved." Heart and mouth, inward belief and outward confession, belong together.

There is no substantive difference between being *justified* and being *saved*. The content of the belief and that of the confession need to be merged. Implicit in the good news are the truths that Jesus Christ died, was raised, was exalted and now reigns as Lord and bestows salvation on those who believe. This is not salvation by slogan but by faith, that is, by an intelligent faith that lays hold of Christ as the crucified and resurrected Lord and Savior.

Anyone and Everyone

ROMANS 10:11-13

> [11]As Scripture says, "Anyone who believes in him will never be put to shame." [12]For there is no difference between Jew and Gentile—the same Lord is Lord of all and richly blesses all who call on him, [13]for, "Everyone who calls on the name of the Lord will be saved."

Christ has come and died, and been raised, and is therefore immediately accessible to faith. We do not need to do anything. Everything that is necessary has already been done. Moreover, because Christ himself is near, the gospel of Christ is also near. It is in the heart and mouth of every believer.

Paul's emphasis is on the close, ready, easy accessibility of Christ and his gospel. He stresses that Christ is not only easily accessible but equally accessible to all, to "anyone" and to "everyone," since "there is no difference," no favoritism.

All three verses here refer to Christ and affirm his availability to faith, although each describes in different terms both the nature of faith and how Christ responds to believers.

First, Paul quotes Isaiah: "Anyone who believes in him will never be put to shame." This is a second quotation of Isaiah 28:16, the first having been in Romans 9:33. Belief and confession are not a mere subscription to a creed; they are a matter of trust in Christ.

Second, there is a marvelous affirmation that through Christ there is no distinction between Jew and Gentile, for "the same Lord is Lord of all and richly blesses all who call on him." All distinctions between those who have been justified by faith and are now in Christ—distinctions not only of race but also of sex and culture—are not abolished (since Jews are still Jews, Gentiles still Gentiles, men still men and women still women), but they are rendered irrelevant.

Third, Paul elaborates both our calling on the Lord and his blessing of us. To "call on him" is more precisely to call "on the name of the Lord," that is, to appeal to him to save us in accordance with who he is and what he has done. "Everyone" who thus calls on him, we are assured, "will be saved." Peter cited this quotation from Joel 2:32 on the day of Pentecost, transferring the text from God to Jesus, which is also what Paul does here.

Then what is necessary to salvation? First, the fact of the historic Jesus Christ, incarnate, crucified, risen, reigning as Lord and accessible. Second, the apostolic gospel, which makes him known. Third, simple trust on the part of the hearers, calling on the name of the Lord, combining faith in the heart and confession with the mouth.

Their Voice Has Gone Out

ROMANS 10:14-15

[14]How, then, can they call on the one they have not believed in? And how can they believe in the one of whom they

have not heard? And how can they hear without someone
preaching to them? [15]And how can anyone preach unless
they are sent? As it is written: "How beautiful are the feet
of those who bring good news!"

In order to demonstrate the indispensable necessity of evangelism,
Paul asks four consecutive questions.

First, in order to be saved, sinners must call on the name of
the Lord. But "how, then, can they call on the one they have not
believed in?" Calling on his name presupposes that they know
and believe his name. This is the only place in Paul's letters
where he uses the term *believe in*, although it is the regular expression in John's writings for saving faith. Here, since saving
faith is presented as "calling on" Christ's name, the kind of belief
Paul has in mind must be the prior stage of believing the facts
about Jesus that are included in his "name."

Second, "how can they believe in the one of whom they have
not heard?" Just as believing is logically prior to calling, so
hearing is logically prior to believing. In other words, people will
not believe Christ until they have heard him speaking through
his messengers or ambassadors.

Third, "how can they hear without someone preaching to
them?" In ancient times, before the development of the mass
media of communication, the major means of transmitting news
was the herald's public proclamations in the city square or the
marketplace. There could be no hearers without heralds.

Fourth, "how can anyone preach unless they are sent?" It is
not clear what kind of sending Paul has in mind. Paul and his
fellow apostles were directly commissioned by Christ. There

were also apostles of the churches, sent out as missionaries. In either case, the need for heralds is now confirmed from Scripture: "As it is written, 'How beautiful are the feet of those who bring good news!'"

The essence of Paul's argument is seen if we put his six verbs in the opposite order: Christ sends heralds, heralds preach, people hear, hearers believe, believers call, and those who call are saved. The relentless logic of Paul's case for evangelism is felt most forcibly when the stages are stated negatively and each is seen to be essential to the next. Unless some people are commissioned for the task, there will be no gospel preachers; unless the gospel is preached, sinners will not hear Christ's message and voice; unless they hear him, they will not believe the truths of his death and resurrection; unless they believe these truths, they will not call on him; and unless they call on his name, they will not be saved.

Who Has Believed?

ROMANS 10:16-19

[16]But not all the Israelites accepted the good news. For Isaiah says, "Lord, who has believed our message?" [17]Consequently, faith comes from hearing the message, and the message is heard through the word about Christ. [18]But I ask: Did they not hear? Of course they did:

"Their voice has gone out into all the earth,
    their words to the ends of the world."

[19]Again I ask: Did Israel not understand? First, Moses says,

> "I will make you envious by those who are not a nation;
>   I will make you angry by a nation that has no
>   understanding."

Preaching leads to hearing, and hearing to believing. Why then have the Israelites not believed? In answer to this perplexing question, Paul ventilates and rejects two possible explanations. Later he will supply his own explanation.

First, "did they not hear?" This is the right first question to ask, since believing depends on hearing. But Paul no sooner asks the question than he summarily dismisses it: "Of course they did." As evidence of this assertion, he quotes Psalm 19:4. His choice of biblical quotation is surprising, since what Psalm 19 celebrates is not the worldwide spread of the gospel but the universal witness of the heavens to their Creator. Paul of course knew this. It seems perfectly reasonable to suggest that he was transferring eloquent biblical language about global witness from the creation to the church, taking the former as symbolic of the latter. If God wants the general revelation of his glory to be universal, how much more must he want the special revelation of his grace to be universal too! So the Jews *have* heard; they cannot blame their not believing on their not hearing.

Second, then, "Did Israel not understand?" We take Paul's point that it is quite possible to hear without understanding, as Jesus warned us in his parable of the sower. But Paul also rejects this explanation of Jewish unbelief and backs up his position by first quoting from Moses. There are people with "no understanding."

But they are not the Jews; they are the Gentiles, whom Moses also describes as "not a nation." God reveals his intention to make Israel both *envious* of and *angry* at the "no nation," "no understanding" Gentiles because of the blessings he would give them.

God Holds Out His Hands

ROMANS 10:20-21

> [20] And Isaiah boldly says,
>
>> "I was found by those who did not seek me;
>>> I revealed myself to those who did not ask for me."
>
> [21] But concerning Israel he says,
>
>> "All day long I have held out my hands
>>> to a disobedient and obstinate people."

If, then, Israel's rejection of the gospel cannot be attributed either to her not hearing it or to her not understanding it, she must be without excuse. This is the third possible explanation of her unbelief, which Paul now accepts. Israel is simply stubborn.

True, the Israelites were ignorant of God's righteousness, but this is now seen to be willful ignorance. They had stumbled over the "stumbling stone," namely, Christ.

In order to enforce this idea, Paul now quotes Isaiah. The prophet's *bold* words prove to come from the lips of God himself. He draws a sharp contrast between the Gentiles and the Jews, his actions toward them and their attitudes toward him.

God deliberately reverses the roles between himself and the Gentiles. It would normally be for them to ask, seek and knock (as

Jesus was later to put it) and to adopt toward him the respectful attitude of a servant at the master's disposal, saying "Here I am." Instead, although they did not ask or seek or offer themselves to God's service, he allowed himself to be found by them, he revealed himself to them, and he even offered himself to them, saying humbly to them, "Here am I." This is dramatic imagery for grace, God taking the initiative to make himself known.

God's initiative to Israel is even more pronounced. He does not simply allow himself to be found; he actively holds out his hands to them. Like a parent inviting a child to come home, offering a hug and a kiss, and promising a welcome, so God has opened and stretched out his arms to his people. He has kept his arms continuously outstretched, all day long, pleading with them to return. But he has received no response. They do not even give him the neutral response of the Gentiles, who decline either to ask or to seek. No, their response is negative, resistant, recalcitrant, dismissive. They are determined to remain a disobedient and obstinate people. We feel God's dismay, his grief.

So Paul concludes his second exploration into the unbelief of Israel. In chapter 9 he attributed it to God's purpose of election, on account of which many were passed by and only a remnant was left, an Israel within Israel. In chapter 10, however, he attributes it to Israel's own disobedience. Their fall was their fault. The paradox between divine sovereignty and human responsibility remains.

Romans 10

....

DISCUSSION GUIDE

OPEN

When have you seen the sadness of a ruptured relationship?

STUDY

Read Romans 10.

1. Focus on verses 1-4. Describe Paul's attitude toward the Jews.

2. What were the strengths and what were the inadequacies of their religion?

3. Paul quotes the teachings of Moses about the law—but he applies those teachings to Jesus (vv. 5-8). What is appealing about "the righteousness that is by faith"?

4. Verses 9-13 contain an ancient creed of the Christian faith. According to these verses, what defines a Christian?

5. What words and phrases in verses 11-13 express the invitation offered by God?

6. How might the message of Romans 10 affect your relationships with other Christians?

7. How might the message of Romans 10 affect your relationships with those who have not yet come to saving faith?

8. Notice the four questions of verses 14-15 and the explanation in verses 16-19. According to these verses, what are the usual steps toward becoming a Christian?

9. Paul quotes Isaiah in verse 15. What is the significance of the quotation in this context?

10. In verses 19-21 Paul again quotes Moses and Isaiah. What do these verses show about God's actions toward people—and their response to him?

11. What do these verses reveal about God's relationship with the Jews?

APPLY

1. Verse 9 says that Christians confess, "Jesus is Lord." Make a mental review of what you have said and done in the last week.

2. In what ways have you confessed that Jesus is your Lord?

3. Verses 14-15 speak of the importance of sharing the good news of Jesus with those who do not yet believe. What can you do to take part in that task?

3

Romans 11
A Deep-Rooted Tree

❧

A Remnant Remains

ROMANS 11:1-6

¹I ask then: Did God reject his people? By no means! I am an Israelite myself, a descendant of Abraham, from the tribe of Benjamin. ²God did not reject his people, whom he foreknew. Don't you know what Scripture says in the passage about Elijah—how he appealed to God against Israel: ³"Lord, they have killed your prophets and torn down your altars; I am the only one left, and they are trying to kill me"? ⁴And what was God's answer to him? "I have reserved for myself seven thousand who have not bowed the knee to Baal." ⁵So too, at the present time there is a remnant chosen by grace. ⁶And if by grace, then it cannot be based on works; if it were, grace would no longer be grace.

One might expect that, since Israel has rejected God, God has rejected them. But they are not the abandoned nation they may seem. Their rejection is only partial; a believing remnant remains. Paul brings forward four pieces of evidence to back up his statement that God has not rejected his people.

The first piece of evidence is personal. Paul himself as a Jew is proof that God has not rejected his people, not even him, the blasphemer and persecutor of Christians. Although he opposed God, God did not reject him.

The second piece of evidence is theological. The apostle has anticipated it in the wording of his question, whether God has rejected "his people," that is, God's special chosen people, the people of his covenant, which he has declared unbreakable. In answering his question he underlines this by describing them as "his people, whom he foreknew." Foreknowledge and rejection are mutually incompatible.

Third, Paul brings forward the biblical evidence of the situation in the time of Elijah. After the prophet's victory over the prophets of Baal at Mount Carmel, he fled from Queen Jezebel into the desert and later took refuge in a cave on Mount Horeb. God told Elijah that he was by no means the sole surviving loyalist. Although the doctrine of the remnant was not developed until Isaiah's time, the faithful remnant already existed during the prophetic ministry of Elijah at least a century earlier.

Paul's fourth evidence that God had not totally rejected his people was contemporary. Just as in Elijah's day there was a remnant of seven thousand, "so too, at the present time," namely, in Paul's day, "there is a remnant." It was probably sizeable. The chief characteristic of this remnant was that it had been "chosen by grace." *Grace* emphasizes that God has called the remnant

grace = relationships

into being, just as he had "reserved" for himself the loyal minority in Elijah's day.

Grace is God's gracious kindness to the undeserving, so that if his election is "by grace, then it cannot be based on works; if it were, grace would no longer be grace." In our era of relativistic fog, it is refreshing to see Paul's resolve to maintain the purity of verbal meanings. His objective is to insist that grace excludes works, that is, God's initiative excludes ours.

A Spirit of Stupor

ROMANS 11:7-12

> [7]What then? What the people of Israel sought so earnestly they did not obtain. The elect among them did, but the others were hardened, [8]as it is written:
>
> > "God gave them a spirit of stupor,
> >> eyes that could not see
> >> and ears that could not hear,
> > to this very day."
>
> [9]And David says:
>
> > "May their table become a snare and a trap,
> >> a stumbling block and a retribution for them.
> > [10]May their eyes be darkened so they cannot see,
> >> and their backs be bent forever."
>
> [11]Again I ask: Did they stumble so as to fall beyond recovery? Not at all! Rather, because of their transgression, salvation has come to the Gentiles to make Israel envious.

¹²But if their transgression means riches for the world, and their loss means riches for the Gentiles, how much greater riches will their full inclusion bring!

How does Paul apply this remnant theology to the facts of his own day and experience? It obliges him to stop generalizing about "Israel" and to make a division. For what Israel "sought so earnestly [presumably righteousness] they did not obtain," at least not as a whole; "but the elect among them did," namely, those who were chosen by grace and so justified by faith. "The others," the unbelieving Israelite majority, "were hardened." There can be little doubt that Paul meant they were hardened by God, since the next verse says that "God gave them a spirit of stupor." Nevertheless, as with the hardening of Pharaoh and those he represented, a judicial process is in mind by which God gives people up to their own stubbornness.

What this *hardening* means in practice Paul goes on to indicate from two Old Testament quotations, both of which refer to eyes that cannot see.

The first quotation is a conflation of Deuteronomy 29:2-4 and Isaiah 29:10. In the Deuteronomy text, Moses tells the Israelites that although they have witnessed God's wonders, yet he has not given them "a mind that understands or eyes that see or ears that hear" (Deuteronomy 29:4). From the Isaiah text Paul quotes only the first sentence, to the effect that God has given them "a spirit of stupor" (or "a deep sleep"), a complete loss of spiritual sensitivity that was self-induced before it became a divine judgment. This condition, Paul adds, continues to afflict Israel to this very day.

Paul's second quotation comes from Psalm 69, which portrays a righteous person's experience of persecution. Early Christians quickly identified this psalm as messianic. This victim of unprovoked hostility prays both that God will vindicate him and that God's just judgment will fall on his enemies. Because of the messianic nature of the psalm, Paul is able to reverse its application. Instead of Israel being the persecuted, it has become (in its rejection of Christ) the persecutor.

So while a believing remnant of Israel remains, the majority are hardened. But the present situation is neither permanent nor hopeless. Israel's fall, which Paul has proved to be not total, is not final either. On the contrary, far from their being on a downward spiral, the spiral is upward. They have not stumbled "so as to fall beyond recovery," but rather to rise, and in that rise both to experience and to cause Gentiles to experience greater blessings than would have been the case if they had not fallen in the first place. Such is God's merciful providence.

A Wild Olive Shoot Grafted In

ROMANS 11:13-21

[13]I am talking to you Gentiles. Inasmuch as I am the apostle to the Gentiles, I take pride in my ministry [14]in the hope that I may somehow arouse my own people to envy and save some of them. [15]For if their rejection brought reconciliation to the world, what will their acceptance be but life from the dead? [16]If the part of the dough offered as firstfruits is holy, then the whole batch is holy; if the root is holy, so are the branches.

[17]If some of the branches have been broken off, and you, though a wild olive shoot, have been grafted in among the others and now share in the nourishing sap from the olive root,[18]do not consider yourself to be superior to those other branches. If you do, consider this: You do not support the root, but the root supports you. [19]You will say then, "Branches were broken off so that I could be grafted in." [20]Granted. But they were broken off because of unbelief, and you stand by faith. Do not be arrogant, but tremble. [21]For if God did not spare the natural branches, he will not spare you either.

Paul's sequence of thought is like a chain with three links. First, through Israel's fall, salvation has already come to the Gentiles. Second, this Gentile salvation will make Israel envious and so lead to Israel's restoration or fullness. Third, Israel's fullness will bring yet much greater riches to the world. Thus the blessing ricochets from Israel to the Gentiles, from the Gentiles back to Israel, and from Israel to the Gentiles again. The first stage has already taken place; it is the ground on which the second and third may confidently be expected to follow.

When Israel sees the blessings of salvation being enjoyed by believing Gentiles, they will covet these blessings for themselves and will repent and believe in Jesus in order to secure them. Thus provoked to a good kind of envy, they will be led to conversion. The salvation enjoyed by Israel will spill over in further blessing to the world.

Paul uses two little metaphors that function like proverbs, one taken from the ceremonial life of Israel, the other from agriculture. Both are clearly intended to justify Paul's confidence in the spread or escalation of blessings he has been describing. As when a representative piece of dough is consecrated to God, the whole belongs to him, so when the first converts believe, the conversion of the rest can be expected to follow. And as the Jewish patriarchs belong to God by covenant, so do their descendants who are included in the covenant. This picture of "root" and "branches" leads Paul to develop his allegory of the olive tree.

The olive, cultivated in groves or orchards throughout Palestine, was an accepted emblem of Israel. Paul develops the metaphor to illustrate his teaching about Jews and Gentiles. The cultivated olive is the people of God, whose root is the patriarchs and whose stem represents the continuity of the centuries. The branches that have been "broken off" stand for the unbelieving Jews who have been temporarily discarded, and the "wild olive shoot," which has been "grafted in among the others," stands for Gentile believers.

The olive has experienced both a pruning and a grafting. Some branches have been cut out of the cultivated tree; that is, some Jews have been rejected. In their place a wild shoot has been grafted in; that is, some Gentiles have believed and have been welcomed into God's covenant people. The caution to believing Gentiles is clear. They should not become arrogant, for it is only "by faith" that they stand.

Hope for Israel

ROMANS 11:22-27

²²Consider therefore the kindness and sternness of God: sternness to those who fell, but kindness to you, provided

that you continue in his kindness. Otherwise, you also will be cut off. [23]And if they do not persist in unbelief, they will be grafted in, for God is able to graft them in again. [24]After all, if you were cut out of an olive tree that is wild by nature, and contrary to nature were grafted into a cultivated olive tree, how much more readily will these, the natural branches, be grafted into their own olive tree!

[25]I do not want you to be ignorant of this mystery, brothers and sisters, so that you may not be conceited: Israel has experienced a hardening in part until the full number of the Gentiles has come in, [26]and in this way all Israel will be saved. As it is written:

"The deliverer will come from Zion;
    he will turn godlessness away from Jacob.
[27]And this is my covenant with them
    when I take away their sins."

Paul presents a warning to Gentile believers and a promise to Jews. If those grafted in could be cut off, then those cut off could be grafted in again. Since the natural branches were broken off, the wild ones could be too. The Gentiles could be rejected like the Jews. There is no room for complacency. And since the wild branches were grafted in, the natural ones could be too. The Jews could be accepted like the Gentiles. There is no room for despair.

Paul now addresses his readers directly, his "brothers and sisters," probably including both Gentile and Jewish church members, since he is now going to refer to the future of both.

What Paul especially wants them to know is "this mystery," not a secret that is known only by the initiated, but a secret that has now been openly revealed and has therefore become public truth. Essentially the mystery is Christ himself. But in particular it is the good news that in Christ, Gentiles are now equal beneficiaries with the Jews of the promises of God and are equal members of God's family.

The mystery consists of three consecutive truths. "Israel has experienced a hardening in part." Paul has already stated this fact, but now he stresses that it is only partial, since not all Israelites have experienced it, and only temporary, since it will last only "until the full number of the Gentiles has come in." While Israel remains hardened and continues to reject Christ, the gospel will be preached throughout the world, and more and more Gentiles will hear and respond to it. "And in this way all Israel will be saved." This "Israel" means ethnic or national Israel, in contrast to the Gentile nations. "All Israel" must mean the great mass of the Jewish people, comprising both the previously hardened majority and the believing minority. It need not mean literally every single Israelite.

What kind of salvation is in view? The scriptural foundation, which Paul now supplies, helps us answer this question. The deliverer would come to bring his people to repentance and so to forgiveness, according to God's covenant promise. The salvation of Israel which Paul has prayed for, to which he will lead his own people by arousing their envy, which has also come to the Gentiles, and which one day all Israel will experience, is salvation from sin through faith in Christ.

God's Mercy for All

ROMANS 11:28-32

> [28]As far as the gospel is concerned, they are enemies for
> your sake; but as far as election is concerned, they are
> loved on account of the patriarchs, [29]for God's gifts and
> his call are irrevocable. [30]Just as you who were at one time
> disobedient to God have now received mercy as a result
> of their disobedience, [31]so they too have now become
> disobedient in order that they too may now receive mercy
> as a result of God's mercy to you. [32]For God has bound
> everyone over to disobedience so that he may have mercy
> on them all.

Paul sums up his argument in two distinct statements, both very
finely chiseled and sculptured. Both focus on still unbelieving
Israel ("they"), although in relation to believing Gentiles ("you").
Both not only describe present reality (which includes continuing Jewish unbelief) but also indicate the grounds for confidence that God has neither rejected his people nor allowed
them to fall beyond recovery. These grounds for confidence are
God's election and God's mercy.

First, God's election is irrevocable. On the one hand, the Jews
are not only rejecting the gospel but actively opposing it and
doing their best to prevent you Gentiles from hearing it. So then,
in relation to the gospel, and for your sake (because God wants
you to hear and believe), he is hostile to them. On the other
hand, the Jews are the chosen, special people of God, the descendants of the noble patriarchs with whom the covenant was made

and to whom the promises were given. So then, in relation to election, and for the sake of the patriarchs (because God is faithful to his covenant and promises), he loves them and is determined to bring them to salvation. For God never goes back on his gifts or his call.

The second ground for confidence that God has a future for his people is his mercy. For God's mercy is shown to the disobedient. Human disobedience and divine mercy are depicted in the experience of both Gentiles and Jews; the obvious difference is that, whereas God has already been merciful to disobedient but repentant Gentiles, his mercy to disobedient Israel belongs largely to the future. It is because of disobedient Israel that disobedient Gentiles have received mercy, and it is because of this mercy to disobedient Gentiles that disobedient Jews will receive mercy too. We again detect the chain of blessing, as Israel's disobedience has led to mercy for the Gentiles, which in turn will lead to mercy for Israel.

Paul has been at pains to argue that there is no distinction between Jews and Gentiles either in sin or in salvation. Now he writes that, as they have been together in the prison of their disobedience, so they will be together in the freedom of God's mercy. Moreover, he has predicted the future fullness both of Israel and of the Gentiles. When these two fullnesses are fused the new humanity will be realized, consisting of huge numbers of the redeemed, the great multinational multitude that no one can count, who were formerly in Adam but are now in Christ, experiencing his overflowing grace and reigning with him in life.

Paul's Doxology

ROMANS 11:33-36

> [33]Oh, the depth of the riches of the wisdom and knowledge of God!
>
> How unsearchable his judgments,
> and his paths beyond tracing out!
> [34]"Who has known the mind of the Lord?
> Or who has been his counselor?"
> [35]"Who has ever given to God,
> that God should repay them?"
> [36]For from him and through him and for him are all things.
> To him be the glory forever! Amen.

Step by step Paul has shown how God has revealed his way of putting sinners right with himself, how Christ died for our sins and was raised for our justification, how we are united with Christ in his death and resurrection, how the Christian life is lived not under the law but in the Spirit, and how God plans to incorporate the fullness of Israel and of the Gentiles into his new community. Paul's horizons are vast, taking in time and eternity, history and eschatology, justification, sanctification and glorification. Now he stops, out of breath. Analysis and argument must give way to adoration.

Paul has already written of God's wealth and the riches that the Lord Jesus bestows indiscriminately on all who call on him. Elsewhere he describes God as "rich in mercy" and refers to Christ's inexhaustible riches. The dominant thought is that salvation is a gift from God's riches and that it immensely enriches those to whom it is given.

Then there is God's wisdom, hidden in Christ, displayed on the cross (though to human beings it appears to be folly) and unfolded in his saving purpose. If the wisdom of God planned salvation, the wealth of God bestows it. God's wealth and wisdom are not merely deep; they are unfathomable. His decisions are unsearchable and his ways inscrutable.

It is ludicrous, as Paul's two Old Testament quotations make clear, to imagine that we could ever teach or give God anything. It would be absurd to claim that we know his mind and have offered him our advice. It would be equally absurd to claim that we have given him a gift and so put him in our debt. We are not God's counselor; he is ours. We are not God's creditor; he is ours. We depend entirely on him to teach and to save us. The initiative in both revelation and redemption lies in his grace.

If we ask where all things came from in the beginning and still come from today, our answer must be "from God." If we ask how all things came into being and remain in being, our answer is "through God." If we ask why everything came into being and where everything is going, our answer must be "for and to God." God is the Creator, Sustainer and Heir of everything, its source, means and goal. He is the Alpha and the Omega, and every letter of the alphabet in between.

It is because all things are from, through and to God that the glory must be his alone. The true knowledge of God will always lead us to worship, as it did Paul. Our place is on our faces before him in adoration.

Romans 11

....

Discussion Guide

OPEN

What are some of your personal "roots" in the Christian faith?

STUDY

Read Romans 11.

1. Verses 1 and 11 voice two questions as an outline to this section of Paul's letter. In view of what Paul has said so far, why are these reasonable questions?

2. Focus on verses 1-10. How might the experience of Elijah be a comfort to Jewish converts to Christianity (vv. 2-5)?

3. How would you describe the tension between grace and works (vv. 5-6)?

4. What do you find troubling in verses 7-10?

5. Focus on verses 11-24. What does the tree with the grafted branches express about the relationships between God, the Jews and the Gentiles?

6. Verse 22 says, "Consider therefore the kindness and sternness of God." Which of these two qualities are you likely to

emphasize over the other? What dangers could this unbalanced emphasis create?

7. Focus on verses 25-32. What reasons for hope do you find here?

8. The mercy of God comes up several times in these verses. In what ways are both Jews and Gentiles recipients of God's mercy?

9. How have you seen God's mercy at work?

10. Study the doxology of verses 33-36. How is God's character reflected in this song of praise?

11. Chapters 9–11 of Romans, often called "the Jewish section," have a long reputation for difficult interpretation. How is this doxology a fitting close to this part of Paul's letter?

APPLY

1. Verse 20 advises readers, "Do not be arrogant, but tremble." What are some ways that you can express appropriate humility about your relationship with God?

2. Verses 11-21 draw a powerful image of an olive tree with a cut-off branch and a wild branch grafted in, drawing life from its deep roots. What strengths can you draw from this root system of the ancient Hebrew faith?

4

Romans 12

Getting Practical

❧

Living Sacrifices

ROMANS 12:1-2

> [1]Therefore, I urge you, brothers and sisters, in view of God's mercy, to offer your bodies as a living sacrifice, holy and pleasing to God—this is your true and proper worship. [2]Do not conform to the pattern of this world, but be transformed by the renewing of your mind. Then you will be able to test and approve what God's will is—his good, pleasing and perfect will.

There is no greater incentive to holy living than a contemplation of the mercy of God. God's grace, far from encouraging or condoning sin, is the spring and foundation of righteous conduct.

In view of God's mercy, Paul makes his ethical appeal. It concerns the presentation of our bodies to God and our transformation by the renewal of our minds. He represents us as a priestly people who, in responsive gratitude for God's mercy, "offer" or present our bodies as living sacrifices, which are both "holy and pleasing to God," the moral equivalents to being physically unblemished or without defect, and a fragrant aroma. Such an offering is "true and proper worship," which could mean either *reasonable* or *rational*. This living sacrifice, this rational, spiritual worship, is not to be offered in the temple courts or in the church building, but rather in home life and in the marketplace. It is the presentation of our bodies to God.

Even today some Christians feel self-conscious about their bodies. The traditional evangelical invitation is that we give our *hearts* to God, not our *bodies*. But no worship is pleasing to God that is purely inward, abstract and mystical; it must express itself in concrete acts of service performed by our bodies.

The second part of Paul's appeal relates to our transformation according to God's will. It is Paul's version of the call to nonconformity and holiness that is addressed to the people of God throughout Scripture. We human beings seem to need a model to copy, and ultimately there are only two. There is "this world," which is passing away, and there is "God's will," which is "good, pleasing and perfect." The change that takes place in the people of God is a fundamental transformation of character and conduct, away from the standards of the world and into the image of Christ himself.

Although Paul does not tell us here how our mind becomes renewed, we know from his other writings that it is by a combination of the Spirit and the Word of God. Certainly regeneration by the Holy Spirit involves the renewal of every part of our humanness, which has been tainted and twisted by the fall, and this includes our mind. But in addition, we need the Word of God, which is the Spirit's "sword," and which acts as an objective revelation of God's will.

Here then are the stages of Christian moral transformation: first our mind is renewed by the Word and Spirit of God; then we are able to discern and desire the will of God; and then we are increasingly transformed by it.

Judging Ourselves Accurately

ROMANS 12:3-5

> ³For by the grace given me I say to every one of you: Do not think of yourself more highly than you ought, but rather think of yourself with sober judgment, in accordance with the faith God has distributed to each of you. ⁴For just as each of us has one body with many members, and these members do not all have the same function, ⁵so in Christ we, though many, form one body, and each member belongs to all the others.

Paul addresses his Roman readers with the self-conscious authority of Christ's apostle. In thinking about ourselves, we must avoid both too high an estimate of ourselves and (Paul might have added) too low an estimate. Instead, and positively, we are to develop "sober judgment." How? First by reference to our faith, and second by reference to our gifts. The standard by which we measure ourselves is the same for all Christians, that is, saving faith in Christ crucified. Only this gospel of the cross can enable us to soberly measure ourselves.

If God's gospel is the first measure by which we should evaluate ourselves, the second is God's gifts. In order to enforce this, Paul draws an analogy between the human body and the Christian community. "Just as each of us has one body with many members, and these members do not all have the same function," although (it is implied) the different functions are necessary for the health and enrichment of the whole, "so in Christ," by our common union with him, "we, though many, form one body."

Although Paul stops short of saying that we are the body of Christ, his assertion that we are "one body in Christ" will have had enormous implications for the multiethnic Christian community in Rome. As one body, "each member belongs to all the others." That is, we are dependent on one another, and the one-anotherness of the Christian fellowship is enhanced by the diversity of our gifts.

This metaphor of the human body, which Paul develops in different ways in different letters, enables him here to hold together the unity of the church, the plurality of the members and the variety of their gifts. The recognition that God is the giver of the gifts is indispensable if we are to make an accurate estimate of ourselves.

A renewed mind is a humble mind like Christ's. Our renewed mind, which is capable of discerning and approving God's will, must also be active in evaluating ourselves, our identity and our gifts. For we need to know who we are, and to have an accurate, balanced and above all sober self-image.

Different Gifts

ROMANS 12:6-8

> [6]We have different gifts, according to the grace given to each of us. If your gift is prophesying, then prophesy in accordance with your faith; [7]if it is serving, then serve; if it is teaching, then teach; [8]if it is to encourage, then give encouragement; if it is giving, then give generously; if it is to lead, do it diligently; if it is to show mercy, do it cheerfully.

Just as God's grace had made Paul an apostle, so his grace bestows different gifts on other members of Christ's body. Paul proceeds to give his readers a sample of seven gifts, which he urges them to exercise conscientiously for the common good. He divides them into two categories, which might be called "speaking gifts" (prophesying, teaching and encouraging) and "service gifts" (serving, contributing, leading and showing mercy).

The first gift Paul mentions here is *prophesying*, that is, speaking under divine inspiration. The remaining six gifts are more mundane. *Serving* is a generic word for a wide variety of ministries, so whatever ministry gift people have been given, they should concentrate on using it. Similarly, teachers should cultivate their *teaching* gift and develop their teaching ministry. *Encouraging* has a wide spectrum of meanings, ranging from encouraging and exhorting to comforting, conciliating or consoling. Personal *giving* is to be done with generosity, without grudging or with sincerity, without ulterior motives. Diligent *leadership* may apply both in the home and in the church. And to show *mercy* is to care for anybody who is in need or in distress.

Moreover, mercy is not to be shown reluctantly or patronizingly, but cheerfully.

This list of seven spiritual gifts in Romans 12 is much less well-known than either the two overlapping lists in 1 Corinthians 12 or the short list of five in Ephesians 4:11. It is important to note both the similarities and the dissimilarities between them.

First, all the lists agree that the source of the gifts is God and his grace, although in Romans it is God the Father, in Ephesians it is God the Son and in 1 Corinthians it is God the Holy Spirit. And being gifts of trinitarian grace, both boasting and envying are excluded. Second, the purpose of the gifts is related to the building up of the body of Christ. Third, all the lists emphasize the variety of the gifts, each seeming to be a random selection. But, whereas students of the 1 Corinthians lists tend to focus on the supernatural (tongues, prophecy, healing and miracles), in Romans 12 all the gifts apart from prophecy are either general and practical (service, teaching, encouragement and leadership) or even prosaic (giving money and doing acts of mercy). It is evident that we need to broaden our understanding of spiritual gifts.

Sincere Love

ROMANS 12:9-12

> [9]Love must be sincere. Hate what is evil; cling to what is good. [10]Be devoted to one another in love. Honor one another above yourselves. [11]Never be lacking in zeal, but keep your spiritual fervor, serving the Lord. [12]Be joyful in hope, patient in affliction, faithful in prayer.

So far in Romans all references to love have been to the love of God, but now Paul focuses on love as the essence of Christian discipleship. Each of his staccato imperatives adds a fresh ingredient to his recipe for love.

Sincerity. "Love must be sincere," that is, "without hypocrisy." The hypocrite was literally the play-actor. The church must not turn itself into a stage. Love is not theater; it belongs to the real world. Indeed love and hypocrisy exclude one another.

Discernment. "Hate what is evil; cling to what is good." It may seem strange that the exhortation to love is followed immediately by a command to hate. But we should not be surprised. For love is not a blind sentiment. On the contrary, it is discerning. It is so passionately devoted to the beloved object that it hates every evil that is incompatible with his or her highest welfare.

Affection. "Be devoted to one another in love." The words Paul uses here were originally applied to blood relationships in the human family. Paul reapplies them to the tender, warm affection that should unite the members of the family of God.

Honor. "Honor one another above yourselves." This is Paul's second "one another" exhortation. Love in the Christian family is to express itself in mutual honor as well as in mutual affection.

Enthusiasm. "Never be lacking in zeal, but keep your spiritual fervor, serving the Lord." Religious enthusiasm is often despised as fanatical. But zeal is fine so long as it is according to knowledge. In telling the Romans to keep their spiritual fervor, Paul is almost certainly referring to the Holy Spirit. Practical commitment to the Lord Jesus, as slave to master, will keep zeal rooted in reality.

Patience. "Be joyful in hope, patient in affliction, faithful in prayer." At the heart of this triplet is the reference to hope, namely, our confident Christian expectation of the Lord's return and the glory to follow. To us this is the source of abiding joy. But it also calls for patience, as meanwhile we endure tribulation and persevere in prayer.

More About Christian Love

ROMANS 12:13-16

¹³Share with the Lord's people who are in need. Practice hospitality.

¹⁴Bless those who persecute you; bless and do not curse. ¹⁵Rejoice with those who rejoice; mourn with those who mourn. ¹⁶Live in harmony with one another. Do not be proud, but be willing to associate with people of low position. Do not be conceited.

Paul continues with his recipe for sincere Christian love.

Generosity. "Share with the Lord's people who are in need." This can mean either to share in people's needs and sufferings or to share our resources with them. We are reminded of the generosity in the early Jerusalem church, whose members shared their possessions with those more needy than themselves.

Hospitality. "Practice hospitality." Love of sisters and brothers in Christ has to be balanced by love of strangers. Hospitality was especially important in Paul's day, since inns were few and far between, and those that existed were often unsafe or unsavory places. It was essential, therefore, for Christian people to open their homes to travelers, and in particular for local church leaders to do so. In fact, Paul did not urge the Romans to "practice" hospitality, but rather to literally "pursue" it.

Good will. "Bless those who persecute you; bless and do not curse." Although our persecutors are outside the Christian community, the call to bless them is a necessary challenge to Christian love. Blessing and cursing are opposites, wishing people respectively good or ill, health or harm. There is no better way to express our positive wishes for our enemies' welfare than to turn them into prayer and into action.

Sympathy. "Rejoice with those who rejoice; mourn with those who mourn." Love never stands aloof from other people's joys or pains. Love identifies with them, sings with them and suffers with them. Love enters deeply into their experiences and their emotions, their laughter and their tears, and feels solidarity with them, whatever their mood.

Harmony. "Live in harmony with one another." The sentence is literally, "Think the same thing toward one another." Since Christians have a renewed mind, it should also be a common mind, sharing the same basic convictions and concerns. Without this common mind we cannot live or work together in harmony.

Humility. "Do not be proud, but be willing to associate with people of low position. Do not be conceited." Snobs are obsessed with questions of status, with the stratification of society into "upper" and "lower" classes or its division into distinctions of tribe and caste, and so with the company they keep. They forget that Jesus fraternized freely and naturally with social rejects and calls his followers to do the same with equal freedom and naturalness.

What a comprehensive picture of Christian love Paul gives us! Love is sincere, discerning, affectionate and respectful. It is both enthusiastic and patient, both generous and hospitable, both benevolent and sympathetic. It is marked by both harmony and humility. Christian churches would be happier communities if we all loved one another like this.

Overcome Evil with Good

ROMANS 12:17-21

[17]Do not repay anyone evil for evil. Be careful to do what is right in the eyes of everyone.[18]If it is possible, as far as it depends on you, live at peace with everyone. [19]Do not take revenge, my dear friends, but leave room for God's wrath, for it is written: "It is mine to avenge; I will repay," says the Lord. [20]On the contrary:

"If your enemy is hungry, feed him;

if he is thirsty, give him something to drink.

In doing this, you will heap burning coals on his head."

[21]Do not be overcome by evil, but overcome evil with good.

The most striking feature of this final paragraph, if we add verse 14, which anticipated it, is that it contains four resounding negative imperatives, all saying the same thing in different words. Retaliation and revenge are absolutely forbidden to the followers of Jesus. And in spite of our inborn retributive tendency, ranging from the child's tit for tat to the adult's more sophisticated determination to get even, Jesus calls us instead to imitate him. He never hit back in either word or deed. There is a place for the punishment of evildoers in the law courts, and Paul will come to that later in Romans. But in personal conduct we are never to get our own back by injuring those who have injured us.

The Christian ethic is never purely negative, however, and each of Paul's four negative imperatives is accompanied by a positive counterpart. If his first antithesis between good and evil was "bless and do not curse," which we have already considered, his second begins: "Do not repay anyone evil for evil." Instead, we are to "be careful to do what is right in the eyes of everyone." It would be inconsistent to refrain from evil if at the same time we are not practicing good.

A further counterpart to retaliation follows, equally universal in its application. "If it is possible, as far as it depends on you, live at peace with everyone." To refuse to repay evil is to refuse to inflame a quarrel. But we also have to take the initiative in positive peacemaking. Sometimes other people are not willing to live at peace with us, or they lay down a condition for reconciliation that would involve an unacceptable moral compromise. We must still make the effort, even if peace is not always possible.

Paul's third prohibition and positive counterpart are "Do not take revenge, my dear friends, but leave room for God's wrath," because vengeance belongs to the Lord. The two activities that are prohibited to us (retaliation and punishment) are now said to belong to God. The reason the repayment or judging of evil is forbidden to us is not that it is wrong in itself (for evil deserves to be punished and should be) but that it is God's prerogative, not ours. We are to allow God's wrath to be expressed through the state's administration of justice.

The two positive alternatives to revenge are to leave any necessary punishment to God and meanwhile to get busy serving our enemy's welfare. These are not contradictory. Our personal responsibility is to love and serve our enemy according to his or her needs and genuinely to seek his or her highest good.

Romans 12

....

DISCUSSION GUIDE

OPEN

In your approach to faith, do you consider yourself more practical or more theoretical? Explain your response.

STUDY

Read Romans 12.

1. Using the content of verses 1-2, describe in your own words an appropriate response to God's mercy.

2. Notice that these verses speak of both mind and body. Why are both of these important in our relationship with God?

3. What are some practical ways that you could offer your body as a living sacrifice to God?

4. In what ways is a group of Christians like a single body? (Compare the word *body* in verses 1, 4 and 5.)

5. Study the list of gifts in verses 6-8. How might each contribute to the well-being of other Christians?

6. What expressions of love do you find in verses 9-16? (Find all that you can.)

7. When has receiving one of the expressions of love described here made a major impact on you?

8. Several times in verses 17-21 Paul uses the words *Do not*. What general themes do you see in what we are *not* to do?

9. Paul follows each use *do not* with what we are to do instead. In view of these instructions, how are we to deal with people who might otherwise be our enemies?

10. It is easy, almost natural, to be "overcome by evil" (v. 21). We simply join what is going on around us. How might following the principles in this passage lead us instead to overcome evil?

11. In what practical ways might Romans 12 help you obey Christ's command to "Love your enemies, do good to those who hate you" (Luke 6:27)?

APPLY

1. Few of us have people we would label as enemies. But most of us have difficult people in our lives, people whose interests and values are so different from our own that we could hardly think of them as friends. Bring to mind one of these people who has particularly made your life difficult.

2. Skim through Romans 12:9-21 with this person in mind. What do you find here that might lead you to "live at peace"?

3. What practical step could you take in that direction?

4. Consider your relationships within your church, fellowship group or family. In view of verses 9-16, what is one way that you could better express your love to one person?

5

Romans 13
Conscientious Citizenship

❧

God-Established Authority

ROMANS 13:1-3

¹Let everyone be subject to the governing authorities, for there is no authority except that which God has established. The authorities that exist have been established by God. ²Consequently, whoever rebels against the authority is rebelling against what God has instituted, and those who do so will bring judgment on themselves. ³For rulers hold no terror for those who do right, but for those who do wrong. Do you want to be free from fear of the one in authority? Then do what is right and you will be commended.

Relations between church and state have been controversial throughout Christian history. The model that accords best with Paul's teaching is partnership, in which church and state recognize and encourage each other's distinct God-given responsibilities in a spirit of constructive collaboration.

What Paul writes here is especially remarkable because at that time there were no Christian authorities (global, regional or local). Authorities were Roman or Jewish, largely unfriendly and even hostile to the church. Yet Paul regarded them as having been established by God, who required Christians to submit to them and cooperate with them.

Paul begins with a clear command of universal application: "Let everyone be subject to the governing authorities." The reason for this requirement is that the state's authority is derived from God. Thus the state is a divine institution with divine authority. Christians are not anarchists or subversives.

We need to be cautious, however, in our interpretation of Paul's statements. He cannot mean that all tyrants have been personally appointed by God, that God is responsible for their behavior or that their authority can never be resisted. Paul means rather that all human authority is derived from God's authority. For example, Pilate misused his authority to condemn Jesus; nevertheless, the authority he used to do this had been delegated to him by God.

Having called for submission, Paul now warns against rebellion. Of course the statement that rulers commend "those who do right" and punish "those who do wrong" is not invariably true. Although Paul had experienced from procurators and centurions the benefits of Roman justice, he also knew about the miscarriage of justice in the condemnation of Jesus. And if all provincial courts were just, he would not have needed to appeal to Caesar. So in depicting rulers in such a good light, as commending the right and opposing the wrong, he is stating the divine ideal, not the human reality.

But if the authority of rulers is derived from God, what happens if they abuse it, if they reverse their God-given duty, commending those who do evil and punishing those who do good? Does the requirement to submit still stand in such a morally perverse situation? No. We are to submit right up to the point where obedience to the state would entail disobedience to God. But if the state commands what God forbids or forbids what God commands, then our plain Christian duty is to resist, not to submit, and to disobey the state in order to obey God.

Whenever laws are enacted that contradict God's law, civil disobedience becomes a Christian duty.

Submit to Authorities

ROMANS 13:4-5

> [4]For the one in authority is God's servant for your good. But if you do wrong, be afraid, for rulers do not bear the sword for no reason. They are God's servants, agents of wrath to bring punishment on the wrongdoer. [5]Therefore, it is necessary to submit to the authorities, not only because of possible punishment but also as a matter of conscience.

Just as he has affirmed three times that the state has authority from God, so now Paul affirms three times that it has a ministry from God. These are significant statements. If we are seeking to develop a balanced biblical understanding of the state, central to it will be the truths that the state's authority and ministry are both given to it by God. Those who serve the state as legislators, civil servants, magistrates, police, social workers or tax collectors are just as much ministers of God as those who serve the church as pastors, teachers, evangelists or administrators.

What is the ministry that God has entrusted to the state? It is concerned with good and evil, which is a recurring theme throughout Romans 12–13. Here, then, are the complementary ministries of the state and its accredited representatives. "The one in authority is God's servant for your good" and "to bring punishment on the wrongdoer." Thus the state's functions are to promote and reward the good and to restrain and punish the evil.

The restraint and punishment of evil are universally recognized as primary responsibilities of the state. When governmental authorities punish evildoers, they are functioning as "servants of God, agents of wrath" on them. God's wrath, which one day will fall on the impenitent and is now seen in the breakdown of the social order, also operates through the processes of law enforcement and the administration of justice. We human beings as private individuals are not authorized to take the law into our own hands and punish offenders. The punishment of evil is God's prerogative, and during the present age he exercises it through the law courts.

In this distinction between the role of the state and that of the individual, we may perhaps say that individuals are to live according to love rather than justice, whereas the state operates according to justice rather than love. This is by no means a wholly satisfactory formula, however, since it sets love and justice over against each other as if they are opposites and alternatives, whereas they do not exclude each other. Even in loving and serving our enemies, we should still be concerned for justice, and we should also remember that love seeks justice for the oppressed. And even in pronouncing sentence, judges should allow justice to be tempered by love, that is, mercy. For evil is not only to be punished; it is to be overcome.

Give What You Owe

ROMANS 13:6-7

> 6This is also why you pay taxes, for the authorities are God's servants, who give their full time to governing. 7Give to everyone what you owe them: If you owe taxes, pay taxes; if revenue, then revenue; if respect, then respect; if honor, then honor.

The role of the state is not only to punish evil but also to promote and reward goodness. This was certainly the case in Paul's day. Yet this positive function of the state is much neglected today. The state tends to be better at punishing than at rewarding, better at enforcing the law than at fostering virtue and service.

Most countries do have some arrangement for recognizing citizens who have made a conspicuous contribution to the public good. They give them a citation or a certificate, a title, a decoration or some other token of appreciation. But they could probably improve and extend their award system, so that only outstanding merit is rewarded, and their honors become increasingly prized and coveted. Perhaps citizens should be given stronger encouragement to recommend people from their community for public recognition.

Paul concludes his section on the state with a reference to the raising and paying of taxes. Taxation was widespread and varied in the ancient world, including a poll tax, land taxes, royalties on farm produce and duty on imports and exports. Paul regarded this topic as coming under the rubric of the ministry of the state.

Political parties differ over the desirable size of the state's role in the nation's life and whether it should increase or decrease taxation. All agree, however, that there are some services the state must provide, that these have to be paid for and that this makes taxes necessary. So Christians should accept their tax liability with good grace, paying their dues in full, both national and local, direct and indirect, and also giving proper esteem to the officials who collect and apply them. Whether "taxes," "revenue," "respect" or "honor," we are to "give to everyone what you owe them."

In this brief passage, Paul gives us a very positive concept of the state. In consequence Christians, who recognize that the state's authority and ministry come from God, will do more than tolerate it as a necessary evil. Conscientious Christian citizens will submit to the state's authority, honor its representatives, pay its taxes and pray for its welfare. They will also encourage the state to fulfill its God-appointed role and, insofar as they have opportunity, actively participate in its work.

Love Fulfills the Law

ROMANS 13:8-10

[8]Let no debt remain outstanding, except the continuing debt to love one another, for whoever loves others has fulfilled the

law. ⁹The commandments, "You shall not commit adultery,"
"You shall not murder," "You shall not steal," "You shall not
covet," and whatever other command there may be, are
summed up in this one command: "Love your neighbor as
yourself." ¹⁰Love does no harm to a neighbor. Therefore love
is the fulfillment of the law.

Paul has just told us to "give to everyone what you owe them"
(v. 7), including paying our debt of taxes. However, there is one
debt that will always remain outstanding, because we can never
pay it, and that is our duty to love. We can never stop loving
somebody and say, "I have loved enough."

If we love our neighbor, at least in the sense of not doing our
neighbor any harm, we may be said to have fulfilled the law even
though we have not fully paid our debt. Paul has already argued
that we are incapable of fulfilling the law by ourselves, on account of our fallen, self-centered nature. But God has done for
us what the law, weakened by our sinful nature, was unable to
do. He has rescued us both from the condemnation of the law
through the death of his Son and from the bondage of the law
by the power of his indwelling Spirit. Now Paul changes his
emphasis from the means of the fulfillment of the law (the Holy
Spirit) to the nature of it (love).

Some people have a naive confidence in love's infallibility. The
truth is that love cannot manage on its own without an objective
moral standard. That is why Paul wrote not that "love is the end
of law" but that "love is the fulfillment of the law." For love and
law need each other. Love needs law for its direction, while law
needs love for its inspiration.

Paul next explains how neighbor love fulfills the law. All God's commandments "are summed up in this one command: 'Love your neighbor as yourself,'" as Jesus had said. It is the essence of love to seek and to serve our neighbor's highest good. That is why "love is the fulfillment of the law."

It is sometimes claimed that the command to love our neighbors as ourselves is a requirement to love ourselves as well as our neighbors. But we can say with assurance that this is not so. Jesus spoke of the first and second commandment without mentioning a third; *agape* is selfless love that cannot be turned in on the self, and according to Scripture, self-love is the essence of sin. Instead, we are to affirm all of ourselves that stems from the creation, while denying all of ourselves that stems from the fall.

What the second commandment requires is that we love our neighbors as much as we do in fact (sinners as we are) love ourselves. If we truly love our neighbors, we will seek their good, not their harm, and we will thereby fulfill the law, even though we will never completely discharge our debt.

Salvation Is Near

ROMANS 13:11-12a

[11]And do this, understanding the present time: The hour has already come for you to wake up from your slumber, because our salvation is nearer now than when we first believed. [12a]The night is nearly over; the day is almost here.

One of the features of our technological society is that we are the slaves of time. We are always checking to know what time it

is and how much time we have before our next appointment or
responsibility.

But it is more important to know God's time, especially "the
present time," the existential moment of opportunity and decision. The Bible divides history into "this age" and "the age to
come," and the New Testament authors are clear that the age to
come or the kingdom of God was inaugurated by Jesus. So at
present the two ages overlap. We are waiting expectantly for the
coming of the Lord, when the old age will finally disappear, the
period of overlap will end, and the new age of God's kingdom
will be consummated. Paul makes three time references, which
assume this background understanding.

First, "the hour has already come" for us to wake up from
slumber. The time for sleep has passed. It is now time to wake up
and get up.

Second, this is "because our salvation is nearer now than
when we first believed." *Salvation* is a comprehensive term, em-
bracing our past (justification), present (sanctification) and
future (glorification). Clearly Paul has in mind our future and
final salvation, which he has earlier depicted in terms of the
freedom of glory, our final adoption as God's children and the
redemption of our bodies. Every day brings it closer.

Third, "the night" (the old age of darkness) is well advanced, so
that it "is nearly over; the day [when Christ returns] is almost
here," on the threshold. Many readers conclude that Paul was
mistaken. The night drags on, and still the day, although it dawned
at Christ's coming, has not yet experienced the fullness of sunrise
at his return. But this is an unnecessary judgment. It is unlikely

that Paul pronounced the end to be imminent, because Jesus had said he did not know the time, the apostles echoed this, and they knew that worldwide evangelization, the restoration of Israel and the apostasy must all precede the final denouement. Also, the apostles knew that the kingdom of God came with Jesus, that the decisive salvation events that established it (his death, resurrection, exaltation and gift of the Spirit) had already taken place, and that God had nothing on his calendar before Christ's second coming. It would be the next and the culminating event.

So the apostles were, and we are, living in "the last days." It is in this sense that Christ is coming "soon." We must be watchful and alert, because we do not know the time. We live in the familiar tension between the "now already" of Christ's first coming and the "not yet" of his second.

Living in the Light

ROMANS 13:12b-14

> 12bSo let us put aside the deeds of darkness and put on the armor of light. 13Let us behave decently, as in the daytime, not in carousing and drunkenness, not in sexual immorality and debauchery, not in dissension and jealousy. 14Rather, clothe yourselves with the Lord Jesus Christ, and do not think about how to gratify the desires of the flesh.

"So" or "therefore" in the middle of verse 12 marks the transition from Paul's statements about the time to his corresponding exhortations. It is not enough to understand the time; we have to behave accordingly.

Paul issues three appeals. The first two include himself ("So let us . . . Let us . . ."), while the third is his direct summons to his readers ("Rather, clothe yourselves"). All three are double sentences, the negative and positive aspects of the appeal forming a radical antithesis.

The first continues the metaphor of night and day, darkness and light. It concerns our clothing, and what (in the light of the time) is appropriate for us to wear. Because of the hour, we must not only wake up and get up, but get dressed as well. We must take off our night clothes, "the deeds of darkness," and put on instead, as suitable daytime equipment for the soldiers of Christ, "the armor of light."

From appropriate clothing, Paul proceeds to appropriate behavior. Positively, "let us behave decently" or becomingly "as in the daytime," that is, as if the day had already dawned, and turn from the kind of things people do under cover of darkness. Opposed to decent Christian behavior is lack of self-control in the areas of drink, sex and social relationships.

Paul's third and concluding antithesis concerns our preoccupation, that which engrosses our attention as Christian people. The alternatives set before us are either the Lord Jesus Christ or our fallen self-centered nature. Clothing ourselves with Christ is something we still have to do or to keep doing. The context suggests that this clothing is for protection rather than adornment. We are to assume not only Christlikeness but Christ himself.

In contrast to the beautiful and protective clothing which is Christ, Paul refers to our ugly, self-centered nature, "the flesh." It has not been eradicated; it is still there. We are told not only to resist gratifying its desires, but not even to "think about how to" do so. Rather we are to be ruthless in repudiating them and putting them to death.

The day of Christ's return is steadily approaching. Our calling is to live in the light of it, to behave in the continuing night as if the day had dawned, to enjoy the "now already" of the inaugurated kingdom in the certain knowledge that what is still "not yet," namely, the consummated kingdom, will soon arrive.

Romans 13

....

DISCUSSION GUIDE

OPEN

What was the attitude toward government in the home where you grew up?

STUDY

Read Romans 13.

1. Verse 1 says that we are to submit to governing authorities. Why? (Find all that you can in vv. 1-7.)

2. Verses 6-7 say that we are to pay our debts. According to this passage, what all might we owe the government?

3. How might the principles of verses 1-7 influence what you say and do during the heat of an election campaign?

4. No government is perfect, and some governments are cruel and corrupt. If you were under a cruel and corrupt government, how could you follow the underlying principles of Romans 13 and still do what is right?

5. We sometimes think of law as being harsh and unyielding, while we see love as soft and flexible. Yet Paul speaks of both

law and love in the same paragraph (vv. 8-10). What connections do you see between love and God's commandments?

6. How might the laws listed here show us practical ways to express love? (Think of tempting situations where these laws would give you guidance toward love.)

7. How can the admonition "Love your neighbor as yourself" (v. 9) lead us toward a godly expression of love for others?

8. According to verses 11-14, how are we to prepare ourselves for Christ's return?

9. What does verse 11 mean by "our salvation is nearer now than when we first believed"?

10. What are some ways that you can "clothe yourselves with the Lord Jesus Christ" (v. 14)?

APPLY

1. We cannot know whether Christ's return will take place in another two thousand years or quite soon. In view of that uncertainty, what kind of person do you want to be when you meet Jesus—whenever that happens?

2. Focus on the command "Love your neighbor as yourself." Consider ways that you express understanding and care for yourself. Next bring to mind a person to whom you ought to be more loving. How might you extend some of those same kindnesses to that person?

6

Romans 14

Living by Someone Else's Rules

❧

Don't Judge Another's Servant

ROMANS 14:1-4

¹Accept the one whose faith is weak, without quarreling over disputable matters. ²One person's faith allows them to eat anything, but another, whose faith is weak, eats only vegetables. ³The one who eats everything must not treat with contempt the one who does not, and the one who does not eat everything must not judge the one who does, for God has accepted them. ⁴Who are you to judge someone else's servant? To their own master, servants stand or fall. And they will stand, for the Lord is able to make them stand.

Paul supplies a lengthy example of what it means in practice to walk according to love. It concerns the relations between two groups in the Christian community in Rome: the weak and the strong. Paul refers to a weakness neither of will nor of character, but of faith. We must not envision a vulnerable Christian easily overcome by temptation, but a sensitive Christian full of indecision and scruples. What the weak lack is not strength of self-control but liberty of conscience.

The most satisfactory identification of the "weak" in Rome is that they were for the most part Jewish Christians whose weakness consisted in their continuing conscientious commitment to Jewish regulations regarding diet and days. Vital to Paul's strategy is his insistence that, from a gospel perspective, questions of diet and days are nonessentials. The Roman issues were "disputable matters" on which it was not necessary for all Christians to agree.

Paul lays down a fundamental principle: "Accept the one whose faith is weak." There is no attempt to conceal or disguise that these brothers and sisters are weak in faith (here meaning "conviction"), immature, untaught and actually mistaken. Yet on that account they are to be neither ignored nor reproached, nor (at least at this stage) corrected, but rather to be received into the fellowship. Such acceptance means to welcome into one's fellowship and into one's heart. It implies the warmth and kindness of genuine love. And it is "without quarreling over disputable matters." Our welcome must include respect for other believers' opinions.

Paul chooses the dietary question as his first illustration of how the weak and the strong, the fearful and the free, should behave toward one another. The weak believer is not a vegetarian on principle or for health, but because the only foolproof way of ensuring that one never eats nonkosher meat is not to eat any meat at all. The reason it is wrong to either despise or condemn fellow Christians is that "God has accepted them." How dare we reject a person whom God has accepted? Indeed, the best way to determine what our attitude to other people should be is to determine God's attitude to them.

If it is inappropriate to reject somebody whom God has welcomed, it is at least as inappropriate to interfere in the relationship between master and servant. We have no business to come between a fellow Christian and Christ, or to usurp Christ's position in the believer's life. "To their own master, servants stand or fall." They are not responsible to us, nor are we responsible for them. "They will stand, for the Lord is able to make them stand." God gives them his approval, whether or not they have ours.

We Belong to the Lord

ROMANS 14:5-9

> [5]One person considers one day more sacred than another; another considers every day alike. Each of them should be fully convinced in their own mind. [6]Whoever regards one day as special does so to the Lord. Whoever eats meat does so to the Lord, for they give thanks to God; and whoever abstains does so to the Lord and gives thanks to God. [7]For none of us lives for ourselves alone, and none of us dies for ourselves alone. [8]If we live, we live for the Lord; and if we die, we die for the Lord. So, whether we live or die, we belong to the Lord. [9]For this very reason, Christ died and returned to life so that he might be the Lord of both the dead and the living.

Paul now develops his second illustration of the relations between the strong and the weak. It concerns the observance or nonobservance of special days, presumably Jewish festivals, whether feasts or fasts, and whether weekly, monthly or annual. Assuming that both weak and strong have reflected on the issue and have reached a firm decision, they will reckon their practice to be part of their Christian discipleship, with the intention of pleasing and honoring the Lord.

Whether one observes special days or regards every day alike, whether one is an eater or an abstainer, the same principles apply. If we are able to receive something from God with thanksgiving, as his gift to us, then we can offer it back as our service to him. The two movements, from him to us and from us to him, belong together and are vital aspects of our Christian discipleship. Both are valuable and practical tests. "Can I thank God for this? Can I do this unto the Lord?"

This introduction of the Lord into our lives applies to every situation. For none of us lives for ourselves alone, and none of us dies for ourselves alone. On the contrary, "if [that is, 'while'] we live, we live for the Lord; and if [that is, 'when') we die, we die for the Lord. So, whether we live or die, we belong to the Lord." Life and death are taken as constituting together the sum total of our human existence. While we continue to live on earth and when through death we begin the life of heaven, everything we have and are belongs to the Lord Jesus and must therefore be lived to his honor and glory.

Why is this? Here is Paul's answer. "For this very reason, Christ died and returned to life so that he might be the Lord of both the dead and the living." It is wonderful that the apostle lifts the very mundane question of our mutual relationships in the Christian community to the high theological level of the death, resurrection and consequent universal lordship of Jesus. Because he is our Lord, we must live for him. Because he is also the Lord of our fellow Christians, we must respect their relationship to him and mind our own business. For he died and rose to be Lord.

No Stumbling Blocks

ROMANS 14:10-13

[10]You, then, why do you judge your brother or sister? Or why do you treat them with contempt? For we will all stand before God's judgment seat. [11]It is written:

"'As surely as I live,' says the Lord,
'every knee will bow before me;
      every tongue will acknowledge God.'"

[12]So then, each of us will give an account of ourselves to God.

[13]Therefore let us stop passing judgment on one another. Instead, make up your mind not to put any stumbling block or obstacle in the way of a brother or sister.

After writing about the strong and the weak, the observers and the abstainers, the living and the dead, all in rather general and impersonal terms, Paul suddenly poses two straight questions in which he sets over against each other "you" and "your brother or sister." Whether we are thinking of the weak with all their tedious doubts and fears, or of the strong with all their brash assurances and freedoms, they are our brothers and sisters. We are related to one another in the strongest possible way, by family ties. When we remember this, our attitude to them becomes at once less critical and impatient, more generous and tender.

We should not judge, because we are going to be judged. What is prohibited to the followers of Jesus is not criticism but censoriousness, "judging" in the sense of passing judgment on or condemning. The reason is that we ourselves will one day appear before the Judge. In other words, we have no warrant to climb onto the bench, place our fellow human beings in the dock and start pronouncing judgment and passing sentence, because God alone is judge and we are not. We will be forcibly reminded of this fact when the roles are reversed.

In order to confirm this, Paul quotes from Isaiah 45:23. The emphasis is on the universality of God's jurisdiction, in that "every knee" and "every tongue" will pay homage to him. "Each of us" individually, not all of us in a mass, "will give an account of ourselves," not of other people, "to God." Because God is the Judge and we are among the judged, "let us stop passing judgment on one another," for then we shall avoid the extreme folly of trying to usurp God's prerogative and anticipate judgment day.

Paul's chief emphasis has been on the Christian responsibility of the strong toward the weak. His argument moves on from how the strong should regard the weak to how they should treat them, that is, from attitudes (not despising or condemning them) to actions (not causing them to stumble or destroying them).

The judgment or decision we are to make is to avoid putting either a hindrance or a snare in any sister's or brother's path, and so causing them to trip and fall.

Righteousness, Peace and Joy

ROMANS 14:14-18

> [14]I am convinced, being fully persuaded in the Lord Jesus, that nothing is unclean in itself. But if anyone regards something as unclean, then for that person it is unclean. [15]If your brother or sister is distressed because of what you eat, you are no longer acting in love. Do not by your eating destroy someone for whom Christ died. [16]Therefore do not let what you know is good be spoken of as evil. [17]For the kingdom of God is not a matter of eating and drinking, but of righteousness, peace and joy in the Holy Spirit, [18]because anyone who serves Christ in this way is pleasing to God and receives human approval.

The strong are convinced that all foods are clean; on the other hand, the weak are convinced that they are not. How should the strong behave when two consciences are in collision?

Paul's response is unambiguous. Although the strong are correct, and he shares their conviction because the Lord Jesus has endorsed it, they must not ride roughshod over the scruples of the weak by imposing their view on them. On the contrary, they must defer to the conscience of the weaker (even though it is mistaken) and not violate it or cause them to violate it. Here is the reason: "If your brother or sister is distressed [feels grief

and even pain] because of what you eat," not only because they
see you doing something they disapprove of but because they
are induced to follow your example against their conscience,
"you are no longer acting in love," no longer walking the path of
love. For love never disregards weak consciences. Instead, love
limits its own liberty out of respect for them.

To wound a weaker brother or sister's conscience is not only
to distress but to "destroy" that person, an action totally incompatible with love. Paul's warning is that the strong who mislead
the weak to go against their consciences will seriously damage
the Christian discipleship of the weak. He urges the strong
against causing such injury to the weak. "Do not let what you
know is good [the liberty you have found in Christ] be spoken
of as evil" because you flaunt it to the detriment of the weak.

If the cross of Christ is the first theological truth that under-
girds Paul's appeal to the strong for restraint, the second is the
kingdom of God, that is, the gracious rule of God through Christ
and by the Spirit in the lives of his people, bringing a free salvation and demanding a radical obedience. Whenever the strong
insist on using their liberty to eat whatever they like, even at the
expense of the welfare of the weak, they are overestimating
the importance of diet (which is trivial) and underestimating the
importance of the kingdom of God (which is central).

"Righteousness, peace and joy" inspired by the Spirit are
sometimes understood as the subjective conditions of being
righteous, peaceful and joyful. But in the wider context of
Romans it is more natural to take them as objective states: justification through Christ, peace with God and rejoicing in hope

of God's glory, of which the Holy Spirit himself is the pledge and foretaste.

Peace and Edification

ROMANS 14:19-21

> [19]Let us therefore make every effort to do what leads to peace and to mutual edification. [20]Do not destroy the work of God for the sake of food. All food is clean, but it is wrong for a person to eat anything that causes someone else to stumble. [21]It is better not to eat meat or drink wine or to do anything else that will cause your brother or sister to fall.

Here Paul repeats, enforces and applies the teaching about proportion or balance that came before. The passage contains three exhortations.

First, "let us therefore make every effort to do [literally, 'let us then pursue'] what leads to peace and to mutual edification." *Peace* here seems to be the *shalom* that is experienced within the Christian community, while *edification* is building one another up in Christ. This is the positive goal that all should seek and that the strong were neglecting in their insensitive treatment of the weak.

Second, "do not destroy the work of God for the sake of food." *The work of God* could mean the individual weaker believer, but in the context it seems to refer to the Christian community. Our responsibility is to seek to build up the fellowship, not to tear it down. Already Paul has used irony to expose the incongruity of valuing food above peace and the health of our stomach above the health of the community; now he does it again Are you strong really prepared, he asks, to demolish God's work "for the sake of food"? There must have been some embarrassed faces among the strong as they listened to Paul's letter being read out in the assembly. His gentle sarcasm showed up their skewed perspective. They would have to reevaluate their values, give up insisting on their liberties at the expense of the welfare of others, and put the cross and the kingdom first.

Paul's third exhortation expresses a contrast between two kinds of behavior. "All food is clean," he affirms, "but it is wrong for a person to eat anything that causes someone else to stumble." This being so, "it is better not to eat meat or drink wine [here mentioned for the first time] or to do anything else that will cause your brother or sister to fall." The statement that "all food is clean" sounds like the slogan of the strong. And Paul agrees with it. Here is the theological truth that gave them their liberty to eat anything they liked. But there were other factors to consider, which would require them to limit the exercise of their liberty. In particular, there was the weaker brother or sister with the oversensitive, overscrupulous conscience, who was convinced that not all food was clean.

So it is wrong for the strong to use their liberty to harm the weak. Alternatively, it is good for the strong to eat no meat and drink no wine, that is, to become vegetarians and total abstainers, and to go to any other extreme of renunciation, if that is necessary to serve the welfare of the weak.

Do All from Faith

ROMANS 14:22-23

> [22]So whatever you believe about these things keep between yourself and God. Blessed is the one who does not condemn himself by what he approves. [23]But whoever has doubts is condemned if they eat, because their eating is not from faith; and everything that does not come from faith is sin.

Paul concludes by drawing a distinction between belief and action, that is, between private conviction and public behavior.

In the private sphere, "whatever you believe about these things," whether you are strong and believe you can eat anything, or weak and believe you cannot, "keep between yourself and God"; keep it a secret. There is no need either to parade your views or to impose them on other people. As for public behavior, there are two options, represented by a strong and a weak Christian. The strong Christian is blessed because his or her conscience approves of eating everything, so that the strong Christian can follow his or her conscience without any guilt feelings. "Blessed is the one who does not condemn himself by what he approves. But whoever has doubts," that is, the weak Christian who is plagued with misgivings because his or her conscience gives vacillating signals, "is condemned if they eat [probably by their conscience, not by God], because their eating is not from faith; and everything that does not come from faith is sin."

Paul's final epigram exalts the significance of our conscience. Although conscience is not infallible, it is nevertheless sacrosanct, so that to go against it (to act "not from faith") is to sin. At the same time, alongside this explicit instruction not to violate our conscience, there is an implicit requirement to educate it.

As in Paul's time, so today we need Christian discernment. Although it is not always easy to distinguish between essentials and nonessentials in Christian doctrine and practice, here is a safe guide. Truths on which Scripture speaks with a clear voice are essentials. Whenever equally biblical Christians, equally anxious to understand and obey Scripture, reach different conclusions, these must be regarded as nonessentials.

In fundamentals, then, faith is primary, and we may not appeal to love as an excuse to deny essential faith. In nonfundamentals, love is primary. Our enthusiasm for the faith is not an excuse for failures in love. Faith instructs our own conscience; love respects the conscience of others. Faith gives liberty; love limits its exercise. No one has put this better than Rupertus Meldenius:

In essentials unity;
In nonessentials liberty;
In all things charity.

Romans 14

....

Discussion Guide

Open

What nonessentials have you seen Christians quibble about? With what results?

Study

Read Romans 14.

1. What "disputable matters" had the potential of dividing the Christians at Rome (vv. 1-8)?

2. What principles here would help us worship together with Christians who disagree on matters that are not essential to the faith?

3. How would you explain that it is right for one Christian to abstain from meat out of service to the Lord while another Christian can eat the same meat and give thanks to God (vv. 6-8)?

4. If you could say with another believer, "Whether we live or die, we belong to the Lord" (v. 8), how would this assurance

affect the way you would handle disagreements with that person? (Consider information in verses 7-11.)

5. Paul says in verse 7, "None of us lives for ourselves alone," yet in verse 12 he says, "Each of us will give an account of ourselves to God." In what practical ways can you live out both this unity and this individuality in your church or fellowship group?

6. Why might a Christian follow someone else's rules, even though those rules are more strict than his or her own? (Draw from throughout verses 13-23.)

7. According to this passage, what are some of the harmful things that can happen if a person who is strong in faith refuses to give in on nonessential matters of conscience?

8. What harm have you seen come from Christian disagreements over minor issues?

9. Study verse 17. What do you see here that might help you through a disagreement with another Christian?

10. Verses 22-23 speak of both freedom and faith. How do you enjoy both of these in your Christian experience?

APPLY

1. What are some of your own "disputable matters," nonessential subjects where some of your Christian friends are more strict than you are?

2. In discussing and acting on those matters, how can you reflect the teachings of Romans 14?

3. Are you being too restrictive in some areas—forcing other Christians to adjust to your limitations?

4. How could you begin to grant your friends freedom and respect in matters that are not central to the Christian faith—and still obey your own conscience?

7

Romans 15

Unity, Liberty and Charity

❦

Build Up Our Neighbors

ROMANS 15:1-4

> ¹We who are strong ought to bear with the failings of the weak and not to please ourselves. ²Each of us should please our neighbors for their good, to build them up. ³For even Christ did not please himself but, as it is written: "The insults of those who insult you have fallen on me." ⁴For everything that was written in the past was written to teach us, so that through the endurance taught in the Scriptures and the encouragement they provide we might have hope.

After identifying himself as one of the "strong," Paul sets forth the Christian responsibility of the strong toward the weak.

First, the strong "ought to bear with the failings [literally 'weaknesses'] of the weak." Strong people are of course tempted to wield their strength to discard or crush the weak. Paul urges them instead to bear with the weak. One person's strength can compensate for another person's weakness.

Second, "we who are strong ought . . . not to please ourselves." To be self-centered and self-seeking is natural to our fallen human nature. But we ought not use our strength to serve our own advantage. As Paul has been arguing, Christians with a strong conscience must not trample on the consciences of the weak.

Third, "each of us should please his neighbors for their good, to build them up." Neighbor pleasing, which Scripture commands, must not be confused with people pleasing, which Scripture condemns. To please people, usually in antithesis to pleasing God, means to flatter people in order to curry favor with them, to win their approval by some unprincipled compromise. That is always incompatible with integrity and sincerity. Perhaps it is to avoid such a possible misunderstanding that Paul qualifies his appeal to please our neighbors with the words "for their good, to build them up." Edification is a constructive alternative to demolition. And this upbuilding of the weak will doubtless include helping to educate and so strengthen their conscience.

But why should we please our neighbor and not ourselves? Because "Christ did not please himself." Although he had the greatest right of all persons to please himself, he instead gave himself in the service of his Father and of human beings.

Instead of referring specifically either to the incarnation or to some incident of Christ's incarnate life, Paul quotes from Psalm 69, which vividly describes the unjust, unreasonable sufferings of a righteous man, and which is quoted of Christ four or five times in the New Testament, being regarded as a messianic prediction.

Christ's fulfillment of Psalm 69:9 leads Paul into a brief digression about the nature and purpose of Old Testament

Scripture. Not only can the Old Testament help teach us about salvation, it can bring us "encouragement" with a view to "endurance," so that "we might have hope," looking beyond time to eternity, beyond present sufferings to future glory. God himself encourages us through the living voice of Scripture. For God continues to speak through what he has spoken.

Accept One Another

ROMANS 15:5-13

[5]May the God who gives endurance and encouragement give you the same attitude of mind toward each other that Christ Jesus had, [6]so that with one mind and one voice you may glorify the God and Father of our Lord Jesus Christ.

[7]Accept one another, then, just as Christ accepted you, in order to bring praise to God. [8]For I tell you that Christ has become a servant of the Jews on behalf of God's truth, so that the promises made to the patriarchs might be confirmed [9]and, moreover, that the Gentiles might glorify God for his mercy. As it is written:

"Therefore I will praise you among the Gentiles;
    I will sing the praises of your name."

[10]Again, it says,

"Rejoice, you Gentiles, with his people."

[11]And again,

"Praise the Lord, all you Gentiles;
    let all the peoples extol him."

[12]And again, Isaiah says,

> "The Root of Jesse will spring up,
>   one who will arise to rule over the nations;
>   in him the Gentiles will hope."

[13]May the God of hope fill you with all joy and peace as you trust in him, so that you may overflow with hope by the power of the Holy Spirit.

Paul's prayer in verses 5-6 can hardly be a plea that the Roman Christians may come to agree with each other about everything, since Paul has been at pains to urge the weak and the strong to accept each other in spite of their conscientious disagreement on secondary matters. It must therefore be a prayer for their unity of mind in essentials. The purpose of this unity of mind is that we may engage in the common worship of God. The one mind is expressed through the one heart and the one mouth; indeed without this unity of mind about Christ, unity of heart and mouth in worship is impossible.

With verse 8 Paul slips almost imperceptibly from the unity of the weak and the strong through Christ to the unity of Jews and Gentiles through the same Christ. In both cases the unity is with a view to worship. Christ's role as the servant of the Jews, that is, as the Jewish Messiah, is seen to have two parallel purposes, first "that the promises made to the patriarchs might be confirmed" and second to incorporate the Gentiles as well. Christ's ministry to the Jews was "on behalf of God's truth," to demonstrate his faithfulness to his covenant promises, whereas his ministry to the Gentiles was on account of "his mercy." It was in mercy to the Gentiles, as it was in faithfulness to Israel, that Christ became a servant for the benefit of both.

Paul has already expressed his assurance that the Scriptures bring us hope. Now he expresses his prayer wish that "the God of hope" may cause the Roman Christians to "overflow with hope." Hope of course always looks to the future. And since Paul has just quoted Isaiah's prophecy that the Messiah will be the object of the Gentiles' hope, we are given a clue as to what hope is in his mind. Paul looks forward to the time when the fullness of both Israel and the Gentiles will have come in, then to the culmination of history with the second coming of Christ, and then beyond it to the glory of the new universe, which Jews and Gentiles will together inherit. Thus joy, peace, faith and hope are essential Christian qualities. If faith is the means to joy and peace, overflowing hope is their consequence, and all four are due to the power of the Holy Spirit within us.

I Glory in Christ

ROMANS 15:14-19a

[14]I myself am convinced, my brothers and sisters, that you yourselves are full of goodness, filled with knowledge and competent to instruct one another. [15]Yet I have written you quite boldly on some points to remind you of them again, because of the grace God gave me [16]to be a minister of Christ Jesus to the Gentiles. He gave me the priestly duty of proclaiming the gospel of God, so that the Gentiles might become an offering acceptable to God, sanctified by the Holy Spirit.

¹⁷Therefore I glory in Christ Jesus in my service to God. ¹⁸I will not venture to speak of anything except what Christ has accomplished through me in leading the Gentiles to obey God by what I have said and done—^{19a}by the power of signs and wonders, through the power of the Spirit of God.

Has Paul been presumptuous to address a church he did not found and has never visited? Has he given the impression that he regards the Romans' Christianity as defective and immature? He expresses his confidence in his readers. But then why has he thought it necessary to write to them as he has done? He supplies two reasons. First, "I have written to you quite boldly on some points to remind you of them again." The apostles had been entrusted with the task of formulating the gospel and laying the foundations of the faith. Consequently, they kept reminding the churches of the original message and calling them back to it. Paul's second reason for writing has to do with his unique ministry as the apostle to the Gentiles. Although he did not found the church in Rome, he has authority to teach its members on account of his special vocation, by God's grace alone, to be the apostle to the Gentiles.

Next Paul elaborates the nature of his ministry. Many readers are surprised that he says he has a "priestly duty," but his vocabulary is unmistakable. Paul regards his missionary work as a priestly ministry because he is able to offer his Gentile converts as a living sacrifice to God. It is not that he enables them to offer themselves to God, for it is Paul himself who presents the sacrifice. Although Gentiles were excluded from the temple in Jerusalem and were not permitted to share in the offering of its sacrifices, now through the gospel they themselves become a holy and acceptable offering to God.

Paul describes the objective of his ministry as being to lead "the Gentiles to obey God." His emphasis here is on obedience rather than faith, presumably because obedience is the indispensable consequence of saving faith. In this ministry Paul refuses to recount his own exploits. All he will dare to talk about is "what Christ has accomplished through me." Paul is not comfortable to think of himself as Christ's partner; he prefers to be Christ's agent or even instrument, so that Christ works not "with" him but "through" him.

Paul refers to the things he has said and done, and to the power of signs and wonders, all done in the Holy Spirit. Yet physical miracles are not the only way the power of the Spirit is displayed. His usual way is through the Word of God. It is he who takes our feeble human words and confirms them with his divine power in the minds, hearts, consciences and wills of the hearers. Every conversion is a power encounter in which the Spirit through the gospel rescues and regenerates sinners.

A Pioneer Ministry

ROMANS 15:19 b-22

[19b]So from Jerusalem all the way around to Illyricum, I have fully proclaimed the gospel of Christ. [20]It has always been my ambition to preach the gospel where Christ was not known, so that I would not be building on someone else's foundation. [21]Rather, as it is written:

"Those who were not told about him will see,
    and those who have not heard will understand."

[22]This is why I have often been hindered from coming to you.

Paul gives a succinct and modest summary of ten years of
strenuous apostolic labor, including his three heroic missionary
journeys. The expression "all the way around" should probably be
translated "in a circle" or "in a circuit." Then one can visualize or
trace on a map the arc of Pauline evangelism encircling the
Eastern Mediterranean. This does not mean that Paul had satu-
rated the whole area with the gospel. His strategy was to evangelize the populous and influential cities and plant churches
there, then leave to others the radiation of the gospel into the
surrounding villages.

Having plotted the sweeping arc that represents his ten years
of missionary outreach, Paul goes on to explain the consistent
pioneer policy that lay behind it. Paul was quite clear in his other
writings that Christ calls different disciples to different tasks
and endows them with different gifts to equip them. His own
calling and gift as apostle to the Gentiles were to pioneer the
evangelization of the Gentile world, and then leave to others,
especially to local, residential leaders, the pastoral care of the
churches. It was in keeping with this policy that, positively, he
would evangelize only "where Christ was not known," and negatively, he would avoid "building on someone else's foundation."

Paul has already written that he had often planned to visit
the Romans but so far has been prevented from doing so. Up
to now he has not divulged what stopped him, but now he does.

It has to do with his mission policy. On the one hand, because he was concentrating on pioneer evangelism elsewhere, he was not free to come to them. On the other hand, because the Roman church had not been founded by him, he did not feel at liberty to come and stay.

Paul finds that Scripture validates his policy of pioneer ministry. He quotes Isaiah, writing about the mission of the Servant of the Lord to sprinkle many nations so that they would see and understand what had not so far been told them. Paul sees Isaiah's prophecy fulfilled in Christ, the true Servant, whom he is proclaiming to the unevangelized.

Travel Plans

ROMANS 15:23-29

[23]But now that there is no more place for me to work in these regions, and since I have been longing for many years to visit you, [24]I plan to do so when I go to Spain. I hope to see you while passing through and to have you assist me on my journey there, after I have enjoyed your company for a while. [25]Now, however, I am on my way to Jerusalem in the service of the Lord's people there. [26]For Macedonia and Achaia were pleased to make a contribution for the poor among the Lord's people in Jerusalem. [27]They were pleased to do it, and indeed they owe it to them. For if the Gentiles have shared in the Jews' spiritual blessings, they owe it to the Jews to share with them their material blessings. [28]So after I have completed this task

and have made sure that they have received this contribution, I will go to Spain and visit you on the way. [29]I know
that when I come to you, I will come in the full measure
of the blessing of Christ.

Paul now looks into the future and confides to the Romans his
travel plans. He specifies three destinations. If he were to make
all these journeys by ship, the first would be at least 800 miles,
the second 1,500 and the third 700, making a minimum total
of 3,000 miles, and many more if he were to travel some of the
way by land rather than sea. When we reflect on the uncer-
tainties and hazards of ancient travel, the almost nonchalant
way Paul announces his intention to undertake these three
voyages is extraordinary.

He plans to visit Rome. Now at last the time seems to be ripe
for his long-awaited, long-postponed visit. When he writes that
"there is no more place for me to work in these regions," he
means that there is no more room in Greece and its environs for
his pioneer church-planting ministry. He has also come to see
his visit to Rome as a stepping-stone to Spain. Perhaps Paul
hopes to establish an ongoing relationship with the Christians
in Rome, so that they will continue to support him. But before
he goes to Rome, he has another journey to make.

He plans to visit Jerusalem. He is already on his way to take
an offering from Christians in Macedonia and Achaia to their
sisters and brothers in need in Jerusalem. Paul had conceived
and initiated this freewill offering project. Clearly he saw great
significance in it, as we see partly from the disproportionate
amount of space he devoted to it in his letters, partly from the

passionate zeal with which he promoted it, and partly from his astonishing decision to add nearly two thousand miles to his journey in order to present the offering himself. This "contribution" was in reality a debt. "For if the Gentiles have shared in the Jews' spiritual blessings, they owe it to the Jews to share with them their material blessings."

He plans to visit Spain. This hope is in keeping with Paul's pioneer mission policy. There were already flourishing Roman colonies in Spain. Did Paul possibly look beyond Spain to the edges of the Roman Empire, to Gaul and Germany, and even to Britain? Whether he reached and evangelized Spain we shall probably never know.

As Paul mentally prepares for his visit to Rome, he is full of assurance. There is no need to detect arrogance in his statement that "I know that when I come to you, I will come in the full measure of the blessing of Christ." Paul's confidence is not in himself but in Christ. It is evident from his request for their prayers that he is not trusting in himself. He knows his weakness, his vulnerability. But he also knows the blessing of Christ.

Join in My Struggle

ROMANS 15:30-32

[30]I urge you, brothers and sisters, by our Lord Jesus Christ and by the love of the Spirit, to join me in my struggle by praying to God for me. [31]Pray that I may be kept safe from the unbelievers in Judea and that the contribution I take to Jerusalem may be favorably received by the Lord's

people there, [32]so that I may come to you with joy, by
God's will, and in your company be refreshed. [33]The God
of peace be with you all. Amen.

Toward the beginning of his letter, Paul assured the Roman
Christians that he was constantly praying for them. So it is entirely appropriate that he should now ask them to pray for him.
He refers to prayer as a "struggle." He is likely thinking of our
need to wrestle with the principalities and powers of darkness.
However, he does not specify any adversary we are to strive with.
It may be that he is simply representing prayer as an activity
demanding great exertion, a struggle with ourselves, in which
we seek to align ourselves with God's will.

Paul asks for their prayers concerning his visits to Jerusalem and
to Rome. With regard to Jerusalem, he mentions two topics for
their prayers, which relate to believers and unbelievers respectively.
He asks the Romans to join him in prayer for his protection and
deliverance from his opponents. He also realizes that it may be
difficult for the believers in Jerusalem to accept the offering from
Gentile believers. In accepting the gift from Paul, Jewish Christian
leaders would be seen to endorse Paul's gospel and his seeming
disregard of Jewish law and traditions. Yet if his offering were to
be rejected, this could cause the rift between Jewish and Gentile
Christians to widen irrevocably. So Paul longs that Jewish-Gentile
solidarity in the body of Christ may be strengthened by the Jewish
Christians' acceptance of its tangible symbol.

Paul now requests prayer also for his visit to Rome. Indeed
he sees the two visits to be inseparably connected. Whatever
reception he is given in Jerusalem, he anticipates that afterward

he will be in need of the joy and refreshment that fellowship with the Roman Christians will bring.

Paul's reference to the will of God in relation to prayer is very significant. The purpose of prayer is emphatically not to bend God's will to ours but rather to align our will to his. The promise that our prayers will be answered is conditional on our asking according to his will. Consequently every prayer we pray should be a variation on the theme "Your will be done."

So prayer is an essential Christian activity, and it is good to ask people to pray for us and with us, as Paul did. But there is nothing automatic about prayer. Praying is not like using a coin-operated machine or a cash dispenser. The struggle involved in prayer lies in the process of coming to discern God's will and to desire it above everything else. Then God will work things out providentially according to his will, for which we have prayed.

Romans 15

....

DISCUSSION GUIDE

OPEN

When have you enjoyed being a small part of something much bigger than you could accomplish alone?

STUDY

Read Romans 15.

1. Romans 15:1 begins with "We who are strong . . ." What responsibilities do Christians who are strong in faith have toward weaker Christians (vv. 1-7)?

2. Why are we told that we are to please our neighbors, not ourselves (vv. 3-4)?

3. Paul offers a prayer for the Roman Christians in verses 5-6 and then instructions in verse 7. According to these verses, what is a healthy church to look like?

4. What connections do you see between healthy human relationships and worship?

5. Note how many times Paul mentions "Gentiles" in verses 8-11. What is the point of this repetition?

6. Focus on Paul's prayer of blessing in verse 13. What in this prayer do you desire for yourself?

7. Describe the assignment God had given to Paul (vv. 15-16).

8. What do you see in Paul's ministry that you would like to imitate in your own work for God? (Consider Paul's attitude as well as his accomplishments.)

9. Why was Paul headed for Jerusalem (vv. 26-29)?

10. What principles regarding the relationship between Christians—even those separated by distance and ideology—are suggested by Paul's benevolent mission to Jerusalem?

11. What instructions for praying does Paul give to his Roman readers (vv. 30-33)?

12. What principles for praying can you gather from these brief instructions?

APPLY

1. With whom do you most need to put to work the principles of unity, liberty and charity described above?

2. What steps can you take in that direction?

3. How can (or does) your own worship reflect the unity and diversity of other Christians?

8

Romans 16
Keeping Friends

❧

Words of Commendation

ROMANS 16:1-5a

[1]I commend to you our sister Phoebe, a deacon of the church in Cenchreae. [2]I ask you to receive her in the Lord in a way worthy of his people and to give her any help she may need from you, for she has been the benefactor of many people, including me. *husband*

[3]Greet Priscilla and Aquila, my co-workers in Christ Jesus. [4]They risked their lives for me. Not only I but all the churches of the Gentiles are grateful to them.

[5a]Greet also the church that meets at their house.

At the end of his letter Paul sends greetings to twenty-six individuals, twenty-four of whom he names, adding in most cases an appreciative personal reference.

Phoebe is mentioned first. It is likely that she was entrusted with the responsibility of carrying Paul's letter to its destination in Rome, although other business was apparently taking her to the city as well. So she needed a letter of commendation to take with her, which would introduce her to the Christians in Rome. Such letters were common in the ancient world and necessary to protect people from charlatans. In his testimonial for Phoebe, Paul asks the Roman church both "to receive her in the Lord," giving her a worthy Christian welcome and hospitality, and "to give her any help she may need" as a stranger in the capital city, presumably in connection with her other business. Phoebe was evidently a woman of means who had used her wealth to support the church and the apostle.

Paul also greets Priscilla and Aquila and the church that meets in their home. Priscilla and Aquila had lived in Italy until the Emperor Claudius expelled the Jews from Rome in AD 49. Then they moved to Corinth, where Paul met them. He worked with them in their tentmaking business, and they traveled with him to Ephesus, which is perhaps where "they risked their lives" for him. Probably after Claudius' death in AD 54 they returned to Rome, which is where they received Paul's greeting. Perhaps a number of other Jewish and Jewish-Christian refugees from Rome met Paul during their exile and returned to Rome after Claudius' edict had been rescinded.

Reflecting on the names and circumstances of the people Paul greets, we should note the unity and the diversity of the church in Rome.

Dear Friends in the Lord

ROMANS 16:5b-10

5bGreet my dear friend Epenetus, who was the first convert to Christ in the province of Asia.

6Greet Mary, who worked very hard for you.

7Greet Andronicus and Junia, my fellow Jews who have been in prison with me. They are outstanding among the apostles, and they were in Christ before I was.

8Greet Ampliatus, my dear friend in the Lord.

9Greet Urbanus, our co-worker in Christ, and my dear friend Stachys.

10Greet Apelles, whose fidelity to Christ has stood the test. Greet those who belong to the household of Aristobulus.

The Roman Christians were diverse in race, rank and gender. As for race, we know already that the church in Rome had both Jewish and Gentile members, and this is confirmed by Paul's list. Certainly Aquila and Priscilla were Jewish Christians, and Paul also refers to "my fellow Jews." But it is equally clear that others on his list were Gentiles.

The social status of Paul's Roman friends is uncertain. On the one hand, inscriptions indicate that some of the names were common names for slaves. On the other hand, some at least were freed people, and others had links with persons of distinction. But the most interesting and instructive aspect of church diversity in Rome is that of gender. Nine out of the twenty-six persons greeted are women, and many of them are commended as hard workers in the Lord's service. The prominent place occupied by women in Paul's entourage shows that he was not at all the male chauvinist of popular fantasy.

Andronicus and Junia were perhaps a married couple, about whom Paul tells us four things: they are his fellow Jews; they have at some point been his fellow prisoners; they were converted before he was; and they "are outstanding among the apostles." In what sense does Paul use the term *apostle*? The most common New Testament application of the word is to the twelve apostles of Christ. Less frequently the term designates "the apostles of the churches." This must have been a considerably larger group, who were sent out by churches as what we would call missionaries. It is in this sense that Andronicus and Junia were outstanding missionaries.

Alongside the Roman church's diversity in race, rank and sex, it experienced a profound unity that transcended its differences.

Greet One Another

ROMANS 16:11-16

¹¹Greet Herodion, my fellow Jew.

Greet those in the household of Narcissus who are in the Lord.

¹²Greet Tryphena and Tryphosa, those women who work hard in the Lord.

Greet my dear friend Persis, another woman who has worked very hard in the Lord.

¹³Greet Rufus, chosen in the Lord, and his mother, who has been a mother to me, too.

¹⁴Greet Asyncritus, Phlegon, Hermes, Patrobas, Hermas and the other brothers and sisters with them.

¹⁵Greet Philologus, Julia, Nereus and his sister, and Olympas and all the Lord's people who are with them.

¹⁶Greet one another with a holy kiss.

All the churches of Christ send greetings.

Paul's list of greetings contains several indications of the fundamental unity of the people of God. Four times he describes his friends as being "in Christ" and five times as "in the Lord." Twice he uses the family language of "sister" and "brother." In addition, he calls people "dear friends." He also mentions two experiences that strengthen Christian unity: being fellow workers and fellow sufferers.

How was the Roman church's unity in diversity displayed in practice? We know that they met in houses or household churches. We cannot suppose that they met according to sex or rank, so that there were different house churches for men and women, for slaves and free. What about race, however? It would be understandable if Jewish Christians and Gentile Christians, and especially the weak and the strong, wanted to meet with their own people, because culture and customs are a strong cement to fellowship. But did they? I do not think so. Toleration of ethnic division in the Roman house churches would be entirely incompatible with Paul's sustained argument in chapters 14-15. How could the church members accept one another, and how could they glorify God together, if they worshiped in different, ethnically segregated house churches? Such an arrangement would contradict the church's unity in diversity.

Paul concludes his list of individual greetings with two universals. The first is that, although only a few of them have been greeted by name, they must all "greet one another with a holy kiss." The logic is that our verbal greeting needs to be confirmed by a visible and tangible gesture, although what form the "kiss" should take will vary according to culture.

Paul's second universal follows: "all the churches of Christ send greetings." How can he speak for all the churches? Is this mere rhetoric? No, he is probably writing representatively. Since he is about to set sail for Jerusalem, we know that those appointed by the churches to carry and deliver the offering have just assembled in Corinth. Perhaps he has asked them if he may send their churches' greetings to Rome.

Unity in diversity is as vital today as in the church in Rome. Of course people like to worship with their own kind, as church growth experts remind us, and it may be necessary to make allowance for different languages, the most formidable barrier of all. But heterogeneity is of the essence of the church, since it is the one and only community in the world in which Christ has broken down all dividing walls.

Watch Out for Divisions

ROMANS 16:17-20

[17]I urge you, brothers and sisters, to watch out for those who cause divisions and put obstacles in your way that are contrary to the teaching you have learned. Keep away from them. [18]For such people are not serving our Lord Christ, but their

own appetites. By smooth talk and flattery they deceive the minds of naive people. [19]Everyone has heard about your obedience, so I rejoice because of you; but I want you to be wise about what is good, and innocent about what is evil.

[20]The God of peace will soon crush Satan under your feet.

The grace of our Lord Jesus be with you.

Some find Paul's transition from greeting to warnings very abrupt and the tone of his admonition so harsh as to be inconsistent with the rest of his letter, especially in view of his gentle handling of the weak. But it is understandable that Paul's mind should move from the Roman church's unity in diversity to the menace of those who were threatening divisions.

Paul issues a threefold appeal—to vigilance, to separation and to discernment.

Some "divisions" are inevitable, like those caused by loyalty to Christ, and so are some "obstacles," especially the stumbling block of the cross. Paul urges the Romans to look out for people who cause either by contradicting the teaching of the apostles. He takes it for granted, even this early in the church's history, that there is a doctrinal and ethical norm the Romans must follow.

Paul calls for separation from those who deliberately depart from the apostolic faith. There is no question of approaching them with a holy kiss, but rather of standing aloof and even turning away. "For such people are not serving our Lord Christ, but their own appetites," literally "their own belly," a graphic metaphor of self-indulgence. These false teachers have no love for Christ and no wish to be his willing slaves. Instead, they are self-centered and have a harmful effect on the gullible.

Paul also urges the Romans to grow in discernment. On the whole he is pleased with their obedience. But there are two kinds of obedience, blind and discerning, and he longs for them to develop the latter. To be "wise about what is good" is to recognize it, love it and follow it. With regard to evil, however, he wants them to be so unsophisticated that they shy away from any experience of it.

Here then are three valuable tests to apply to different systems of doctrine and ethics—biblical, Christological and moral. We can put them in the form of questions about any kind of teaching we encounter. Does it agree with Scripture? Does it glorify the Lord Christ? Does it promote goodness?

Paul adds an assurance to his warning. He wants the Roman Christians to know that there is no doubt about the ultimate triumph of good over evil. He detects the strategy of Satan behind the activity of the false teachers, and he is confident that the devil will be overthrown. It may seem strange that in this context Paul refers to "the God of peace," since enjoying peace and crushing Satan do not sound compatible. But God's peace allows no appeasement of the devil. It is only through the destruction of evil that true peace can be attained. And such victory is impossible apart from "the grace of our Lord Jesus."

Greetings to the Romans

ROMANS 16:21-23

[21]Timothy, my co-worker, sends his greetings to you, as do Lucius, Jason and Sosipater, my fellow Jews.

²²I, Tertius, who wrote down this letter, greet you in the Lord.

²³Gaius, whose hospitality I and the whole church here enjoy, sends you his greetings.

Erastus, who is the city's director of public works, and our brother Quartus send you their greetings.

Having sent his own personal greetings to twenty-six individuals in Rome, Paul now passes on messages from eight named people who are with him in Corinth. He begins with one extremely well-known name, followed by three apparently unknown ones.

If anybody deserved to be called Paul's "co-worker," that person was Timothy. For the last eight years Timothy had been Paul's constant traveling companion and had undertaken several special missions at Paul's request. The apostle evidently had a warm affection for his young assistant. Having led him to Christ, he regarded him as his son in the faith. He was now in Corinth, about to set sail for Jerusalem with the offering from the Greek churches.

From his co-worker Paul turns to three of his fellow Jews. We cannot for certain identify any of them, although many guesses have been made, some more plausible than others. It is tempting to identify Lucius as Luke the evangelist, since we know from one of his telltale "we" passages in Acts that he was in Corinth at the time. The only difficulty is that Luke was a Gentile. But then "my fellow Jews" could refer only to Jason and Sosipater. This Jason could quite easily be the Jason who had been Paul's landlord in Thessalonica, and Sosipater could be the Berean church's delegate to Jerusalem, whose name was abbreviated to Sopater, for he too was in Corinth at the time.

At this point Paul allows his scribe, to whom he has been dictating this letter, to write his own greeting.

Next comes a message from Gaius, Paul's host in Corinth. Several men called Gaius appear in the New Testament, for it was a common name. It would be natural, however, to identify this one with the Corinthian whom Paul had baptized. Some scholars have further suggested that his full Roman name was Gaius Titius Justus, in which case he had a large house next to the synagogue, which he had welcomed Paul into after the Jews had rejected his gospel. It is understandable that Paul would again be his house guest and that the church would also meet in his home.

Two further people complete the series of messages from Corinth. Erastus was a responsible local government official, and Quartus is identified only as "our brother."

It would be a mistake to gloss over this part of Romans as only a list of names. Paul's list of those who send or receive greetings represent Christian fellowship across geographic and cultural distances.

Glory to God Through Jesus

ROMANS 16:25-27

25Now to him who is able to establish you in accordance with my gospel, the message I proclaim about Jesus Christ, in keeping with the revelation of the mystery hidden for long ages past, 26but now revealed and made known through the prophetic writings by the command of the eternal God, so that all the Gentiles might come to the

obedience that comes from faith—[27]to the only wise God
be glory forever through Jesus Christ! Amen.

It can hardly be an accident that Romans begins and ends with
a reference to the power of God through the gospel. If the
gospel is God's power to save, it is also God's power to "establish," which is a term for nurturing new converts and
strengthening young churches. The vision summoned by the
doxology's opening words is of God's ability to establish the
multiethnic church in Rome and to strengthen its members in
truth, holiness and unity.

Paul affirms that God's power to establish the church is in
accordance with "my gospel, the message I proclaim about Jesus
Christ." He can call it "my gospel" because it was revealed and
entrusted to him by God. The "mystery" is a truth or cluster of
truths "hidden for long ages past, but now revealed." God's
secret, hitherto concealed but now revealed, is essentially Jesus
Christ himself in his fullness, and in particular Christ for and in
the Gentiles, so that Gentiles now have an equal share with
Israel in God's promise. The mystery also includes good news
for Jews as well as Gentiles. And it looks forward to the future
glory, when God will bring all things together under one head,
Christ. Thus the mystery begins, continues and ends with Christ.

It is important to grasp that Paul is stating three truths about
the mystery, summed up by the verbs *hidden*, *revealed* and *made
known*. It is not just that the mystery was long concealed and
has now been revealed through the life, death, resurrection and
exaltation of Jesus. This good news must be, and is already being,
made known throughout the world.

Paul concludes with praise for "the only wise God." God's wisdom is seen in Christ himself, above all in his cross which, though foolish to human beings, is the wisdom of God, in God's decision to save the world not through its own wisdom but through the folly of the gospel, in the extraordinary phenomenon of the emerging multiracial, multicultural church, and in his purpose ultimately to unite everything under Christ. No wonder Paul has already broken out in praise of God's wisdom: "Oh, the depth of the riches of the wisdom and knowledge of God!" (Romans 11:33). No wonder he does it again at the end of his letter. Indeed, God's redeemed people will spend eternity worshiping him for his power and wisdom displayed in salvation.

Romans 16

....

Discussion Guide

OPEN

Describe one of your longstanding friendships.

STUDY

Read Romans 16.

1. Study the list of twenty-six people in verses 1-16. What does the list reveal about the way Paul conducted his relationships?

2. Notice the phrases Paul uses to describe his friends. What are some ways that he gives a sense of dignity to his friends even in a mere greeting?

3. What indications do you see of diversity among the people Paul felt close to? (If necessary, do a little research about names and backgrounds in this list.)

4. What concepts expressed in this list of greetings show an undergirding unity within that diversity?

5. What do you see in the relationships implied by Paul's greetings that you would like to incorporate into your own friendships?

6. What last-minute warnings did Paul write in verses 17-19?

7. In practical terms, what does it mean to be wise about what is good and innocent about what is evil?

8. How can we go about achieving that wisdom and innocence?

9. Not only does Paul send greetings to his friends in Rome; he also sends greetings from eight of the friends who are with him. What additional information do you gain here about Paul's circle of friends (vv. 21-23)?

10. Study Paul's closing prayer of praise in verses 25-27. What words and phrases here echo previous segments of Paul's letter?

11. Paul's prayer begins with the statement that God is able to "establish" us by the gospel. In what ways does the book of Romans establish your faith?

APPLY

1. Bring to mind a dozen or so of your friends, neighbors and coworkers. Follow Paul's example and give a brief summary of what you appreciate about each. (Try to find an opportunity to mention your appreciation to them in person.)

2. Paul closes his letter with a prayer of praise for God's wisdom and a desire for God's eternal glory. What are some ways that you have seen God's glory revealed in your friends? In your own experience?

Guidelines for Leaders

My grace is sufficient for you.

2 Corinthians 12:9

If leading a small group is something new for you, don't worry. These sessions are designed to flow naturally and be led easily. You may even find that the studies seem to lead themselves!

This study guide is flexible. You can use it with a variety of groups—students, professionals, coworkers, friends, neighborhood or church groups. Each study takes forty-five to sixty minutes in a group setting.

You don't need to be an expert on the Bible or a trained teacher to lead a small group. These guides are designed to facilitate a group's discussion, not a leader's presentation. Guiding group members to discover together what the Bible has to say and to listen together for God's guidance will help them remember much more than a lecture would.

There are some important facts to know about group dynamics and encouraging discussion. The suggestions that follow should equip you to effectively and enjoyably fulfill your role as leader.

PREPARING FOR THE STUDY

1. Ask God to help you understand and apply the passage in your own life. Unless this happens, you will not be prepared to lead others. Pray too for the various members of the group. Ask God to open your hearts to the message of his Word and motivate you to action.

2. Read the introduction to the entire guide to get an overview of the topics that will be explored. *The Message of Romans* will give you more detailed information on the text. This can help you deal with answers to tough questions about the text and its context that could come up in discussion.

3. As you begin each study, read and reread the assigned Bible passage to familiarize yourself with it.

4. Carefully work through each question in the study. Spend time in meditation and reflection as you consider how to respond.

5. Write your thoughts and responses. This will help you to express your understanding of the passage clearly.

6. It may help to have a Bible dictionary handy. Use it to look up any unfamiliar words, names or places.

7. Reflect seriously on how you need to apply the Scripture to your life. Remember that the group members will follow

your lead in responding to the studies. They will not go any deeper than you do.

LEADING THE STUDY

1. At the beginning of your first time together, explain that these studies are meant to be discussions, not lectures. Encourage the members of the group to participate. However, do not put pressure on those who may be hesitant to speak—especially during the first few sessions.

2. Be sure that everyone in your group has a book. Encourage the group to prepare beforehand for each discussion by reading the introduction to the book and the readings for each section.

3. Begin each study on time. Open with prayer, asking God to help the group to understand and apply the passage.

4. Discuss the "Open" question before the Bible passage is read. The "Open" question introduces the theme of the study and helps group members begin to open up, and can reveal where our thoughts and feelings need to be transformed by Scripture. Reading the passage first could tend to color the honest reactions people might otherwise give—because they are, of course, supposed to think the way the Bible does. Encourage as many members as possible to respond to the "Open" question, and be ready to get the discussion going with your own response.

5. Have a group member read aloud the passage to be studied as indicated in the guide.

6. The study questions are designed to be read aloud just as they are written. You may, however, prefer to express them in your own words. There may be times when it is appropriate to deviate from the discussion guide. For example, a question may have already been answered. If so, move on to the next question. Or someone may raise an important question not covered in the guide. Take time to discuss it, but try to keep the group from going off on tangents.

7. Avoid answering your own questions. An eager group quickly becomes passive and silent if members think the leader will do most of the talking. If necessary, repeat or rephrase the question until it is clearly understood, or refer to the commentary woven into the guide to clarify the context or meaning.

8. Don't be afraid of silence in response to the discussion questions. People may need time to think about the question before formulating their answers.

9. Don't be content with just one answer. Ask, "What do the rest of you think?" or "Anything else?" until several people have given answers to the question.

10. Try to be affirming whenever possible. Affirm participation. Never reject an answer; if it is clearly off-base, ask, "Which verse led you to that conclusion?" or again, "What do the rest of you think?"

11. Don't expect every answer to be addressed to you, even though this will probably happen at first. As group members

become more at ease, they will begin to truly interact with each other. This is one sign of healthy discussion.

12. Don't be afraid of controversy. It can be very stimulating. If you don't resolve an issue completely, don't be frustrated. Explain that the group will move on and God may enlighten all of you in later sessions.

13. Periodically summarize what the group has said about the passage. This helps to draw together the various ideas mentioned and gives continuity to the study. But don't preach.

14. Conclude your time together with prayer, asking for God's help in following through on the applications you've identified.

15. End on time.

Many more suggestions and helps for studying a passage or guiding discussion can be found in *How to Lead a LifeGuide Bible Study* and *The Big Book on Small Groups* (both from InterVarsity Press).

Reading the Bible with John Stott

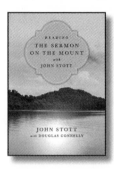

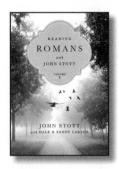

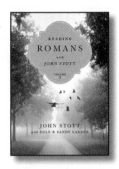

Reading the Sermon on the Mount with John Stott
978-0-8308-3193-7

Reading Romans with John Stott, volume 1
978-0-8308-3191-3

Reading Romans with John Stott, volume 2
978-0-8308-3192-0

Also Available

The Message of Romans
978-0-8308-1246-2